SEEKING GOD'S FACE

Faith in an Age of Perplexity

NOTTO R. THELLE

Translated by Brian McNeil

Paulist Press
New York/Mahwah, NJ

First published as *Ditt ansikt søker jeg,* Oriens Forlag (Oslo) 1993.
Translated with the financial assistance of the Areopagos Foundation.
Most biblical texts are taken from the New Revised Standard Version, Oxford
University Press, 1989. Occasionally, translation is made directly from the orig-
inal texts, to bring out the author's point.

Cover design by Sharyn Banks
Book design by Lynn Else

The picture on the cover is by the Japanese artist Sadao Watanabe and shows
the encounter between Jesus and the Samaritan woman at Jacob's well (see page
9). Watanabe is internationally known for his original use of Japanese artistic
expressions for biblical motives.

Library of Congress Cataloging-in-Publication Data

Thelle, Notto R., 1941–
    [Ditt ansikt søkeroker jeg. English]
    Seeking God's face : faith in an age of perplexity / Notto R. Thelle ; trans-
lated by Brian McNeil.
       p. cm.
    Includes bibliographical references.
    ISBN 978-0-8091-4515-7 (alk. paper)
    1. God (Christianity) 2. Spirituality. I. Title.
    BT103.T4513 2008
    231.7—dc22

                                                          2008001024

Published by Paulist Press
997 Macarthur Boulevard
Mahwah, New Jersey 07430

www.paulistpress.com

Printed and bound in the
United States of America

CONTENTS

CONTENTS

TOWARD A GREATER FAITH

A greater faith is a faith that does not close the borders: on the contrary, it opens them. A greater faith perceives the Creator's presence everywhere—is not the artist recognized in his work? He breathes on us, so that we may live. Should we not then expect that we would become aware of *him*, when life breathes more deeply, and the heart beats faster?

I have reflected on these ideas in my book *Who Can Stop the Wind? (Hvem kan stoppe vinden?)*,[1] which describes my wanderings in the religious landscape of the Far East and at the same time speaks of the rediscovery of the immense and fascinating landscape of Christianity. My conclusion was that we need a faith large enough to encompass human life in all its contradictory variety.

This conclusion was not a full stop, not a period, but rather a colon: this book, *Seeking God's Face*, is an attempt to continue my wanderings. Its main subject is our search for God. Is it possible to get beyond the distorted images and empty words, and find the God who is a living reality? Indeed, can we speak of God at all? I am convinced that it is more important today than ever before to search for the true image of the Godhead, and I attempt to portray some of that God's aspects here.

But I write about other "faces" as well. The one who seeks God is compelled to seek his or her own face too. And in the course of this journey, one stands face-to-face with people who unveil new dimensions of the landscape of faith—challenging, magnificent, and beautiful.

Many of the chapters in this book are inspired by texts of scripture. Some began as sermons and subsequently took the form of essays or brief prose texts. My intention was not to explain the texts and then "apply" them to our own age. I have heard any number of glib "applications" that allegedly make scripture relevant to our contemporary life—and none of these has convinced me that this is the right path to take! Instead, I have tried to let the texts live, so that they disclose themselves in landscapes where the individual can breathe freely and find orientation, without the sensation of being imprisoned. My dream is to help the readers rejoice in the variety of the landscape, so that they will discover what makes sense to them and freely choose the path they take.

This openness and freedom are to be found in the Gospel itself. They were lived by the Master himself, who portrayed the face of God by meeting human beings where they actually were—not where they ought to have been.

I

THE LIGHT
OF THE FACE

The Lord make his face to shine upon you...
(Numbers 6:25)

Faith only comes when we stand face to face—
the ineffable in us with the ineffable beyond us—
suffer ourselves to be seen, to commune,
to receive a ray and to reflect it.
But to do that
the soul must be alive within the mind...
(Abraham Heschel)

I Seek Your Face

I had followed the stream of pilgrims to one of Japan's sacred mountains. Centuries of coming and going had worn the stone slabs and steps to a round smoothness. When at last we reached the summit, we stood in front of the sanctuary, which was mirrored in a still pool under ancient cedar trees. The doors were open. Figures clothed in white bowed in adoration, and we heard, from within, a monotonous chanting sustained by the deep rhythm of the blows struck on a wooden fish. Three hundred years ago, in a similar situation, the poet Basho wrote: "To say more about the sanctuary would be to violate its holiness."

The picture of the sanctuary reflected in the pool confirmed an ancient insight: we see the divine mystery only as a reflection of a still deeper reality. As Paul writes, "Now we see in a mirror, dimly" (1 Cor 13:12). We seek the divinity, but we do not see it clearly. We perceive a presence, but not a presence we could ever explain. We build sanctuaries to house our longings. But we have only veiled and obscure glimpses of the mystery itself. Will we ever see it face-to-face?

The pool concealed secrets of its own. Hundreds of bronze mirrors, which earlier pilgrims had thrown into the pool, had been fished up from the bottom. These were votive gifts from women who were not allowed to ascend the mountain; women were thought to be impure, so that their presence would violate the sanctity of the place. The mirrors were thus a substitute for their presence in person.

I picture a woman concentrating intensely, so that her image will be left indelibly printed on the mirror that she sends to the sanctuary. A few weeks later, it is thrown into the pool and shatters the glittering surface of the water: a mirror meets a mirror. The face is wiped off the bronze mirror and sinks into the pool, which is a mirror image of the sanctuary.

Was this, perhaps, a kind of presence? At any rate, the custom was a beautiful expression of the woman's longing to be there in person. But was it too distant to be able to touch her real life? If she was truly to perceive the presence, it was not enough to entrust the image of her face to a mirror! She had to be there herself, to see and take in everything with her senses. She had to show her face in the sanctuary.

Encountering the Japanese sanctuary reminded me of what a Jewish poet wrote about seeking God. These words are found in the Book of Psalms, written in a different age and a different culture, but they express the same human experiences. If God has created the human person to seek him, why then does he hide his face?

> Hear, O LORD, when I cry aloud,
> be gracious to me and answer me!
> "Come," my heart says, "seek his face!"
>
> Your face, LORD, do I seek.
> Do not hide your face from me.

And sometimes, it is God who addresses to us this prayer: "Do not hide your face! It is *your* face that I seek…" (Ps 27:7–8). This longing cannot be satisfied by means of fleeting images in a bronze mirror. We must show our face, we must dare to let ourselves be seen. And we ourselves must see and hear and take in everything with our senses—with faces uncovered. For we perceive God's presence only when we ourselves are present in our own lives.

This duality is one reason for our unrest. Some people look for God, but find no answer until they dare to look for themselves. Some people try desperately to find their own selves, but they have no success until they begin to ask where God is.

Without this duality, our longing can be obliterated by a spirituality that is remote from our own lives, or stagnate in an isolated self-absorption.

Faith means practicing a life lived face-to-face.

The Burning Blush

"Faith is a blush in the presence of God," according to the Jewish philosopher Abraham Heschel (in *Man Is Not Alone*).[1] God is a lover who longs and searches for the one he loves. He does not want to be alone, and the human person cannot forever remain untouched by God's approaches. "Those of us who cannot keep their striving back find themselves at times within the sight of the unseen and become aglow with its rays. Some of us blush, others wear a mask. Faith is a blush in the presence of God."

But something must happen in our lives before we can reach this point. Heschel continues: "We all wear so much mental make-up, we have almost forfeited our face. But faith only comes when we stand face-to-face—the ineffable in us with the ineffable beyond us—suffer ourselves to be seen, to commune, to receive a ray and to reflect it. But to do that the soul must be alive within the mind."

What is the burning blush?

Most of us associate blushing with a feeling of shame, with the humiliating experience of being found out. We stand unprotected in the presence of one who suddenly has the advantage of us, so we lower our gaze and hide our face—or else we cover ourselves with masks and show another face. But our blush betrays us.

In some forms of faith, the feeling of shame is decisively important. A well-known Norwegian hymn says: "I stand before God who knows all things, and lower my gaze in utter shame." Certainly, such words *can* be the expression of a healthy realism on the part of the believer: when our deepest thoughts are uncovered, we have good reason to lower our gaze. But if the feeling of shame becomes dominant, we end up in a paralyzing self-contempt. Many forms of Christianity have exaggerated the role played by shame in the life of faith.

Blushing is in fact connected with a whole range of feelings. Our cheeks blush when our heart beats faster and life pulsates more quickly through our veins. People blush not only out of shame, but also when they are honored; we blush in rage and in admiration. We blush when we are overwhelmed by joy, or when music and dance sweep us off our feet. And above all, we blush in the presence of love—look at the infant in its mother's arms, look at the parents who blush with pride in their children. Look at children at play, look at people in love when they meet each other, look at friends and married couples who are warmed by each other's presence. We drop our mutual defenses and become aglow with each other's rays.

When people stand before God and blush, it is because they have dared to put aside the masks: they are themselves, they stand there with open faces and feel the touch of love. One of the psalms of David says: "I am continually with you; you hold my right hand...And there is nothing on earth that I desire other than you" (Ps 73:23, 25). It is not by chance that the Bible employs the poetry of love when it speaks of the relationship between God and the human person.

We know a little about human intimacy, and we long for the warmth we receive from others. Do we know anything about God's presence? Perhaps we do long for him, perhaps we take some stumbling steps toward him. Can we believe that he will respond to our approaches? Do we know what it is to recognize the burning blush in God's presence?

I knew a young man who was forever falling in love, but had little self-confidence. He was terribly shy, for he never dared to believe that anyone would respond to his love. Was there anything in him worthy of a woman's favor?

One day, he met a girl—they shook hands, they looked at each other, and something happened between them. Before this, he had loved in secret, from a distance. Now he began to be courageous. He turned up in places where he knew she would be—quite by chance, of course—and they exchanged a few words. They put on a little show for each other, because their feelings had to be camouflaged at all costs. Neither of them should get the impression that something important was at stake! No, it was just nice to be in the same place; they sort of bumped into one another and took the same path home. He found it almost impossible to believe that she was responding to his shy advances. Up to now, he had confided his innermost thoughts only to his diary, in a secret code, but now he found clumsy words to express his feelings: "I like you! You're great!" And finally he found the overwhelming words that he could speak only when all the masks fell away, and he stood there in the open, blushing and unprotected: "I love you!"

Many years later, a new longing began to glow. He was a preacher, and spoke about God. It was his task to lead others to faith, but one day he realized that he did not know what this actually meant: he read the texts and expounded their contents, but they amounted to nothing more than literature—beautiful but unreal. He found the words about God's presence inspiring, but did he know what they meant? He talked about God, but did he know God?

One day, after preaching about "loving God," he wrote in his diary:

> How can you speak about God when you yourself are desperately crying out in the search for him? I spoke about the text: "You shall love the Lord your God with all your heart and all your soul and all your mind and all your strength…" I talked about the wholehearted faith that loves God without worry or reservation—but also about the love that seeks God, the disbelieving, doubting love on the part of those who love a God they do not see, but long for. Love has many forms. One who disbelieves and doubts, but commits his whole person to the search for God, loves God with all his heart. I think the parish got the point. They listened in deep concentration. Only, they did not know that I was talking about myself.

But something happened in him, something that reminded him of how he had first approached the girl he loved. He had loved God at a distance, uncertain and full of doubts. He had immured himself in his longing, fearful that he might betray himself, afraid to put the matter to the test—for then he might be disappointed.

One day, the longing grew so intense that he became courageous. He dared to emerge from the sphere of his loneliness and to draw near to God. He took a few steps, and God came to meet him. His questing eyes saw glimpses of God's presence.

Surely this is what many people experience. God draws near in their lives, in a fleeting encounter that gives them a glimpse of a reality they cannot completely explain. They are touched by something that awakens all their senses to life.

The longing takes control of their lives. They begin to search, they visit places where they have heard God is to be found. They read the Bible—just a little, of course, and quite by chance—

and they dip into books about faith. They go to a concert in a church now and then, or visit a church in some foreign country when they are on vacation. They make their shy advances—there is nothing extraordinary going on here, of course! And yet...

And yet! In their depths, they have a great yearning. They fumble, like people who have just fallen in love. They are terrified of betraying their feelings and being disappointed. But they cannot stop their clumsy advances. One day, they stand blushing before God, and discover that there is an answer to their longings.

"Faith only comes when we stand face-to-face—the ineffable in us with the ineffable beyond us—suffer ourselves to be seen, to commune, to receive a ray and to reflect it. But to do that the soul must be alive within the mind...Faith is a blush in the presence of God."

A Finger Pointing to the Heart

Few pictures have fascinated me as strongly as the Japanese artist Sadao Watanabe's depiction of the encounter between Jesus and the Samaritan woman at Jacob's well (see the cover of this book).[2] With a few rough lines, his composition creates a unity out of the two figures. Jesus and the woman stand on either side of the well and are framed in an arch of light—or perhaps streams of water. The intimacy and warmth of the narrative can be felt across all the chronological and cultural distance.

A simple conversation about water awakens the thirst for life-giving springs: "Everyone who drinks of this water will be thirsty again," says Jesus, "but those who drink of the water that I will give them will never be thirsty. The water that I will give will become in them a spring of water gushing up to eternal life." The woman says to him, "Sir, give me this water, so that I may never be thirsty or have to keep coming here to draw water."

Jesus says to her, "Go, call your husband, and come back." The woman answers him, "I have no husband." Jesus says to her, "You are right in saying, 'I have no husband'; for you have had five husbands, and the one you have now is not your husband. What you have said is true!"

The movement in Watanabe's picture makes toward the center, where an immensely long finger points to the woman's face. She turns away because she cannot bear to meet his gaze. The finger uncovers her secret shame and touches her open wounds. "You have had five husbands, and the one you have now is not your husband." Just one short sentence, and the woman recognizes that he knows her through and through. She tells her friends, "Come and see a man who told me everything I have ever done!" He has seen the face behind the masks, and he expects her to stand upright and meet his gaze (John 4:13–18, 28–29).

A finger has the potential of life and death.

Death—the judging finger that points and sends rays of poison into a wounded person. The lifted finger that coldly confirms the judgment someone has already pronounced over his or her own self. The imperious finger that awaits a service the other person does not wish to perform.

Life—finding an unforgettable expression in Michelangelo's masterly picture of the creation in the Sistine chapel: God's creating finger tenderly touches Adam's powerless hand, and gives him a life and a soul. When Jesus's finger reaches out to the Samaritan woman, the Creator touches a wounded and powerless person: "Live!"

I have seen a finger that created life in other people. An encouragement directed to someone who was on the point of giving up altogether. A question that kindled longing. Or perhaps a reminder: "Do you really want to do what you are doing right now?" Someone had the courage to see them, and they let themselves be seen. The light was restored to their faces. They were touched, and life pulsated with a stronger and freer rhythm.

I have seen the finger in my own life. Friends who understood more than I did pointed, and the creative forces broke loose. The clearest occasion was when an unknown man pointed at the right moment. He belonged to another faith, but had the grace and gift of seeing something of other people's inner thoughts. He told me about my life, about my crises and my longings. We did not speak at great length, but I met someone "who told me everything I had ever done." He did not attempt to make me his disciple; he simply opened my eyes, so that I could see both myself and Christ more clearly. And that gave me a glimpse of how God works in this world.

I have also seen the finger in the many years in which I had contact with Zen Buddhism in Japan. In Zen, the truth is communicated directly "from heart to heart"—but this is not some cheap insight. Zen can seem both cold and brutal, and the meditation demands discipline and perseverance. In dialogue, the master points. His finger becomes a sword that cuts away all our defense mechanisms and glib explanations. The masks must fall, the camouflage must disappear. Ruthlessly, he leads us into the crisis and despair where there is no longer anything to hold onto. Pious words and elegant formulations wither and die. He wants to penetrate to the person behind the masks, and to tear down the façades that hide reality. When at last the face is uncovered and unprotected, the master raises his finger and points at the original face, the naked heart. Only the one who loses himself can find himself.

Jesus pointed to the Samaritan woman and cut through layer upon layer of defense mechanisms: pride and shame, hatred and hypocrisy, daydreams and nightmares, remembrances of embraces and of pain. The mask cracks and a human face comes to light. It is ravaged, marked by life, without makeup, soiled by tears and grief. But it bears the future, because it is the woman's own face.

The encounter with the Master is the hour in which she is born. She herself is both the mother who gives birth and the child who is born. She is now discovering what the Creator had wanted her to be. A Zen Buddhist would perhaps speak of "the face she had before she was born."

She turns her face to the Master, and has nothing to hide. She has come back to the starting point, and life begins anew—because he lifted his finger and touched her with the creative word.

The Face of Blessing

A face speaks. It tells the story of a person's life, and perhaps that is why an old person's face can be so appallingly ugly, or so beautiful. Everything he or she has experienced is etched in a network of wrinkles that reveal new secrets in various situations.

We encounter harsh faces and mild faces. Some are open and confident, others are closed. Faces can be bashful or quick to laugh, greedy or angry, impertinent or dreaming. Some faces are distorted by fear; sickness and desperation cast their own shadows. A poet has spoken of "the line of pain," which is eternally beautiful. In other faces, we see the delicate traces left by joy.

In most people, these traits are interwoven. A face creased in grief can unfold in a smile that tells us that joy lies hidden in the pain. A face that laughs can suddenly open up to reveal chasms of despair. We can of course put on a false face, but pretense too leaves its traces, and the face tells this truth precisely by stiffening into a mask. The faces we encounter display myriad variations on the great themes of life.

We are surrounded by faces from the time we leave our mother's womb until we say farewell to those who surround us. This is a part of what it is to be human—faces meet us, faces turn away. Kindness may shine out, or else we may see the dark radiation of hatred. The face speaks a powerful language!

This may be why the Bible pronounces a blessing by speaking of God's face: "The Lord make his face to shine upon you! The Lord lift up his countenance upon you!" These words have been spoken every single day for almost three thousand years, from one generation to the next.

These words of blessing are alive. They create what they pronounce: light and presence.

When I think back, I see how often we as parents have stood beside our children—when they were newborn, toddlers, teenagers, adults—in a thousand situations where we were overwhelmed by joy and pride. How our faces shone! Of course, anger and irritation could make our faces cloud over, and then we turned hard and cold faces on those we loved most dearly. But the point is that we are familiar with the light of the face.

We see this light around us, too. We have all seen the radiance of a mother giving her child the breast, or a father playing with his children. We see the light in those who meet the person they love. We notice the vibrations between old friends when they talk. There is peace. They lift their faces, and their eyes meet. They share good words with one another. There is blessing.

A few years ago, I came across a poem called "If I Really Cared about You." It was illustrated by pictures of two friends talking together. Their hands reach out to one another and their eyes meet. They have light in their faces:

> If I really cared about you...
> I would look into your eyes when you talk to me,
> I would think about what you had said,
> rather than about what I was going to say when you
>   stopped talking,
> I would listen to your feelings, along with your words

If I really cared about you...
I would laugh with you, not at you,
I would talk with you, not to you,
and I would know when it was time to keep silence

If I really cared about you...
I would not clamber over your walls.
I would wait outside until you let me in by the door.
I would not break the locks guarding your secrets,
I would wait until you gave me the key

If I really cared about you...
I would love you whatever happened,
but I would ask for the best you can give
and cautiously coax it forth from you.[3]

These words about friendship apply also to God's blessing. When God lets his face shine upon us, he does not force his way into our lives; but he is close at hand and speaks good words to us. He does not nag until he gets a place in our hearts: he lifts his face and waits until we stand upright and meet his gaze. He knocks at the door, but he waits outside until we open. He knows the secrets of our lives, but he does not make use of them against us; he waits until we ourselves give him the keys. He loves us whatever happens, and attempts with tremendous caution to coax forth from us the best we can give.

The Gospel tells us that "no one has ever seen God." Our darkened gaze cannot see him. Nevertheless, we have seen his face. He drew the veil aside in one human being, who was his authentic image.

I am sure that Jesus's face was marked by the people he met. He wept with those who grieved, and laughed with those who rejoiced. His eyes saw, and he took people into his own life. Their sorrows and joys left their traces upon him, but the light of his face was not extinguished. He has the features of the God who lifts his face and is near.

God is sometimes called "the ancient of days." His old face is perfect in its beauty, for it is marked by all the joy and pain of the world, but it is purified and made utterly radiant by the flame of love.

One day, we shall see him face-to-face. Until then, we speak the words of blessing, and we are sure that his presence shines upon us. He lifts his face upon us and waits. With tremendous caution, he wants to coax forth the light on our faces, and to bring forth in us the best we have.

The One Who Is Upright

Two biblical motifs are woven together in a pattern that cannot be worn out: God and the human person. The warp that runs through the fabric is God's greatness. "God alone is great," says the prophet. "Holy is his name," says Mary. And as the shuttle runs back and forth, so the human person in the Bible is formed in the great tapestry. Many are surprised to see that it is not the smallness of the human person that is depicted there. Rather, we see images of human beings who walk upright upon God's earth.

A profound biblical insight is that the one who bows down before the greatness of God also becomes a great and complete human being. We tell about God's greatness by straightening up, and stretching our limbs and bodies to the full.

Our vocation is not to be cowed, to go around with necks bowed and eyes fixed on the ground, for then we stagnate—we simply stop growing. Nor is it our vocation to go around on tip-toe, reaching out for something that is higher than we are, for that leads only to overexertion—we stiffen convulsively, or else we trample on other people in our efforts to reach our goal. In other words, we are either "more" than human or "less" than human. But the real challenge is to become a human being who lives at his or her own true height.

Many other movements are involved too, since the human person is not rigidly upright like a statue. We kneel, we bow down, we throw ourselves to the ground, aware that we are formed of dust and will return to dust. We stretch out our hands to heaven, giving expression to our despair or our expectancy. We walk in processions, we sit in silent meditation, or we lean over books in which we can find clearer ideas and better words. The body knows many languages.

But we never stop our movement: we get up from our prayer and our books, we are sent out at the end of worship in church. We stand up and raise our eyes. This is not simply because we are *homo erectus,* the species of animal that stands up and walks on two legs. It is intimately connected with our nature, with our place in God's world. God's grace is expressed in the body's language as the freedom to walk upright. His grace allows us to encounter the new day with our senses open, with unaverted gaze, meeting other faces and stretching out our hands. There is nothing more natural than this, but for some reason it is very difficult!

Think of all those people in the Gospel who literally "got up and walked." A lame man shoulders his bundle and goes to meet life. One who is paralyzed straightens a bent back and aching limbs. A woman who has been defiled gets up and has no need to feel shame when she looks at men. Lepers stretch out their hands and embrace those whom they love. Poor people stand up and speak their names with pride. Sinners emerge from their hiding places and back alleys, their eyes radiant with light. God created us as upright human beings.

With its grim realism, the Bible has more to say about a deformed greatness and a crushed smallness than about straightened backs—it depicts a world where true humanity is under constant threat. The deformed greatness is usually linked to power and wealth, but piety too can become deformed, especially when it is united to power. The Bible describes mighty men who outgrow their God-given size by sucking out the strength of those who are small. It talks about "a man's proud eyes," about "arrogance and haughtiness," about "fatness"—and this language also implies the existence of the nameless ones who bend their backs, crouching and waiting for a blow to fall. They are cast aside and trampled upon, but they are created for something else. Those who are great and proud will fall, and those who are crushed will straighten their backs. This is why the prophet speaks of God's judgment on those who are great and proud (Isa 2:12–17):

> For the LORD of hosts has a day
> against all that is proud and lofty,
> against all that is lifted up and high;
> against all the cedars of Lebanon,
> lofty and lifted up;
> and against all the oaks of Bashan;
> against all the high mountains,
> and against all the lofty hills;
> against every high tower,
> and against every fortified wall;
> against all the ships of Tarshish,
> and against all the beautiful craft.
> The haughtiness of people shall be humbled,
> and the pride of everyone shall be brought low;
> and the LORD alone will be exalted on that day.

Do such bitter words contain any "Gospel"? Is the divine superpower "better" than human power? Some who read these words will feel the noose tightening around their necks—their own self-contempt is enough for them to cope with, and it does not need to draw extra nourishment from the idea of a superpowerful God. They do not need a zealous Lord in heaven who crushes all those who refuse to stay within the normal human limits. And does not the idea that God alone is great recall the charge Ibsen leveled at his contemporaries: "While about one thing alone they're united/namely that greatness be stoned and despited"?

In the Bible, the praise of God's greatness is also a profession of faith in the dignity of the human person, a defense of human greatness. God—who is highest of all—bows down the one who is arrogant, so that others can stand upright. The human dream of "greatness" makes one a rebel against God and an oppressor of other human beings and of the world that God has created. The one who is consumed by arrogance has use for God or other people only as "growth hormones" to promote his own development.

This is why all that is proud and great must disappear: it has grown out of all proportion, like the giant "cedars of Lebanon" that supply no light or life to other plants and finally crash to the ground, brought down by their own arrogant hypertrophy; or like the "high tower and fortified wall," perhaps originally meant to provide protection, but built at the cost of the lives and possessions of the poor and leading only to war and violence. All that is proud and great must disappear, because it destroys the equilibrium in society—like the mighty "ships of Tarshish and all the beautiful craft" that bring wealth and honor to the few, while the mass of the people die nameless and hungry.

It may be that most of us think of Mary as a humble handmaid, a rather pale and lifeless character, but she uses strong words to express the same theme: her God is the Lord, "and holy is his name." He is "the Mighty One [who] has done great things" and has "looked…on the lowliness of his servant," but her awareness of God's greatness does not make her crawl on the ground: she straightens her back and says something that few women have ever dared to say, "From now on all generations will call me blessed." Her God has "scattered the proud in the thoughts of their hearts…[and] brought down the powerful from their thrones." He has "lifted up the lowly…[and] filled the hungry with good things, and sent the rich away empty." He "has done great things for me!" (Luke 1:46–55).

The Bible's words about the human person who stands upright are both judgment and promise: judgment, because arrogance must be broken and wealth and power must be taken from us, in order to make us more whole; and promise, because we shall receive the freedom to straighten our backs and live out our God-given potential.

Our faith that God alone is great opens up a world large enough to let the human person stand upright and reach his or her full height on the earth God has created. There is nothing crawling or crushed about faith; still less does faith mean that we have to grit our teeth and trample on others in our effort to reach unattainable goals.

We were created to stand upright. That is Christianity; that is the Gospel.

Vaults behind Vaults

In the half-darkness of the mighty Romanesque church
the tourists thronged—
vaults behind vaults, no way to take in everything at one
     glance.
A few candle flames flickered.
A faceless angel embraced me
and his whisper ran through all my body:
"Don't be ashamed of being human—be proud!
Within you, there opens up an endless series of vaults
     behind vaults.
You never reach the end; and that is how it should be."
My tears blinded me
and the throng pushed me out onto the piazza
in the baking sunshine along with Mr. and Mrs. Jones,

Mr. Tanaka and Signora Sabatini
and within all of them,
there opened up an endless series of vaults behind vaults.[4]

In his "Romanesque Vaults" (1989), the Swedish poet Tomas
Tranströmer beckons us into the sanctuary with him. Just as we
see one vault after another opening up along the great nave, this
poem too has dimensions that open up when we enter it.

The tourist group has reached the halfway point in its program. They have seen numerous churches and ruins, museums
and art exhibitions. They have haggled in the markets and pushed
their way through the crowds in narrow streets. Some have ven-
tured on romantic escapades, making conquests or else accepting
defeat. And they are beginning to get bored.

Not another church! Explanations and anecdotes once
again—the guide is repeating himself, droning on about historical contexts, artistic styles. Notice the Romanesque architecture,
the supple forms, so solid and feminine! Arches and pillars rise up
and support the roof, like the firmament of heaven, although the
thick walls remind us that everything is firmly planted on earth.
The building is a monument to an age when faith was secure, a
fortress in an uncertain world.

The group begins to get tired. Their thoughts are already en
route to the picturesque restaurant. They get out their cameras,
because they need some photographs for their families and
friends. They walk quickly up to the chancel to get one last
impression—the play of light and darkness, the scent of incense,
the echoes of a far-off Gregorian chant. It is good to experience
this atmosphere, before returning to the grayness of everyday life.

And suddenly, something happens. The music takes hold of
the poet, the light penetrates his skin, he is overwhelmed and
taken captive by the church in which he stands. He had wandered
around, looking at things and taking photographs, but now he
feels he is the one being looked at. He is touched by something

he cannot explain, a presence that makes *him* present. The vaults open up, one after another. He stands on the threshold of something unknown—and yet not foreign. In one sense, he has not moved; but in reality, he has moved out of the tourists' world into a larger universe. The walls, the pillars, the vaults do not form a closed world: here, he sees with open eyes something so hard to grasp outside this church, namely that God's presence pervades the whole world.

In his mind's eye, he sees the generations that built the sanctuary many hundreds of years ago. They staked out a few square meters of the universe, quarried stones out of the earth and the mountains, and built the walls, the pillars, and the vaults. They created a space to house the mystery. They knew that God cannot be held captive in human buildings or thoughts, but they needed signs of his presence—signs that their senses could perceive: the Word that tells about the heart that beats in the universe; bread and wine; the fellowship in a meal that gives strength and nourishment; glowing pictures in glass and lead that give our faith colors; music that makes the soul rejoice and lifts it up in praise of God.

They did not erect the walls to shut God inside and say that he is only here, not outside. No, they wanted to create a meeting place with the one who fills all things with his presence. The sanctuary is a miniature universe, with heaven and earth symbolically built into the vertical axis of the architecture, and with time and eternity as the horizontal axis of the church leading up to the altar. What happens here is not taking place in some remote corner of reality: here, reality itself takes on a new density in the divine presence, and the one who meets God in the sanctuary will find it easier to recognize him outside it.

But something else happens too. Not only are Tranströmer's eyes opened to the symbolism in the gigantic architecture of the church: the inner universe opens up. An angel embraces him and whispers words about human greatness that make his whole body tremble: "Don't be ashamed of being human—be proud! / Within you, there opens up an endless series of vaults behind vaults. / You never reach the end; and that is how it should be."

Today, we have searched out the unknown and made the world our own possession; the human mind has become an object of research, something we have attempted to explain and understand. Longings and urges must be dredged up to the surface; religion has been declared an illusion or a neurotic aggression, God an oppressive father figure. Piece by piece, the strange mechanisms that form the human person have been uncovered—the labyrinths of the mind within us, the complicated role-playing and power games in human society. One could easily believe that there was no hidden vault left to investigate.

As the outer and the inner universes were conquered, the world shrank and ceased to be a land of promise. Paradoxically, when the human person grew in stature and became lord of the world, we became lonely and homeless.

The encounter with mystery places the human being in a larger context: we acquire a new kind of presence within ourselves, and the inner cosmos reawakens. Immanuel Kant once said that two things terrified him: the starry sky above him, and the moral law within him. Perhaps we can adapt these words to speak of the starry sky above us and the starry sky within us, the external sphere with its "vaults behind vaults, no way to take in everything at one glance," and the inner universe with its unimagined dimensions. "You never reach the end; and that is how it should be."

But Tranströmer's eye sees even further than this. When the tourist is swept away by his feelings, this is not just a passing mood. He is overwhelmed and meets the others outside on the piazza, blinded by tears and dazzled by the sunlight, but his eyes remain open. The mystery has given him a new view of existence outside the sacred room.

Sometimes we speak of things as *profane*—literally, "outside the sanctuary." The tourists emerge from the dark church and find themselves once again on the busy piazza. Will the sunlight now reveal the unreality of the romantic feelings in which they had indulged in the "half-darkness" of the church? It would not take much to reduce one's fellow tourists to boring and trouble-some—and basically ordinary—people!

But the opposite happens. Mr. and Mrs. Jones were always loquacious tourists, and that is still the case; Mr. Tanaka is just as punctilious and polite as he was before. As for Signora Sabatini, will anyone ever get a glimpse of what lies behind the façade of her makeup? But suddenly, behind these prosaic faces, Tranströmer sees unknown depths of meaning: "and within all of them, / there opened up an endless series of vaults behind vaults."

The true mystery is not found only within the sanctuary. There, it may indeed exist in a stronger form; it finds expression in the clear, symbolic language of the architecture, with "an end-less series of vaults behind vaults." These signs interpret it, and the atmosphere of the church allows us to breathe it in. But if it does not survive in the profane sphere outside the sanctuary, it is not a genuine mystery—only an agreeable mood.

The one who has perceived the depths in the vaults of the sanctuary, with "no way to take in everything at one glance," is open to the mystery that is found *precisely* in the profane every-day light of the piazza.

Is It Blasphemous to Speak about God?

Few persons in the twentieth century could match the strength and beauty with which the Jewish philosopher Martin Buber made faith come alive. He claims that the human person is essen-tially created for dialogue: we become truly human when we speak with each other, face-to-face. And dialogue with God is necessary, to prevent human dialogue from losing its meaning.

This is why Buber's writings have an intensely personal character—they are like a continuous dialogue. In everything he wrote, we notice the presence of an invisible guest. But faith cannot be taken for granted, and when Buber speaks of God, he must struggle to let the words come alive.

In one of his books, *The Eclipse of God*,[5] he tells about a conversation with a good friend. Buber had read aloud the foreword to his new book, in which—as always—he wrote about his faith in God. After a while, the friend was seized by holy wrath and asked how Buber could keep on saying the word *God*—how could he use such a word about a reality that knows no boundaries, a word so misused, soiled, and profaned! The glitter has worn off that word, thanks to all the innocent blood shed for the sake of God's name—its meaning has been effaced by so much injustice. When the name *God* is applied to the Highest One, this verges on blasphemy.

A silence fell over the room.

Yes, Buber replied after a pause, the word *God* is indeed mutilated and soiled. But that is precisely why we must not abandon it! Generations have laid the burdens of their anxious lives upon this word and weighted it down, so that it cannot rise from the earth, but lies in the dust and bears all their burdens. They draw caricatures and write "God" underneath them. They murder one another and say "in God's name."

But when all madness and blindness turn to dust, and they stand before him in the loneliest darkness, no longer saying "He, He," but rather sighing "Thou," shouting "Thou!" and at the same time saying "God," is it not the living God whom they all implore, the One Living God who *hears* them?

The word *God* is not redeemed by our silence, claims Buber. *We* cannot purify it or restore it to its integrity. But "defiled and mutilated as it is, we can raise it from the ground and set it over an hour of great care."

The Cross in the Wings

In a newspaper portrait of the Swedish entertainer Ernst Rolf, his Norwegian colleague Dag Frøland writes that Rolf "made Scandinavia sing, whistle, and hum." This article, written with great affection, gives the reader a glimpse of a religious dimension in Rolf's life of which few people were aware.

"Every night, before he went on stage to sing 'Better and Better, Day by Day,' he made the sign of the cross in the wings," writes Frøland. "His song is still sung today. Maybe we too should make the sign of the cross before we sing it."

Did Ernst Rolf need the strength—whether great or small—that faith gives? Did the sign of the cross he made in the wings remind him of the pain that lies concealed behind even the most cheerful songs we sing? We need not speculate about such questions; it is enough if this little story shows us something of the deeper dimension underlying the optimism in his cheerful cabaret song. Would not our lives be richer if we too quietly made the sign of the cross—and were aware of what that sign signifies?

Every time I enter St. Olav's chapel in the psychiatric hospital at Modum Bad near Oslo, I am struck by the simple symbolism in its interior. There is no reredos with a picture, as is usual in Norwegian Lutheran churches. Instead, the room opens out upon the wood and the meadows that surround the chapel. The only thing that interrupts the view through the clear glass windows is a wooden cross, superimposed on the world that lies outside.

And surely that is a very accurate picture of our world, for it seems that, in one way or another, everything that lives is marked by the sign of the cross. The cross represents pain, screams, punishment, torture, blood, ugliness; but through Jesus's death, the cross has also become the foremost sign of the love that not only endures and sacrifices, but also transforms and creates anew.

The church speaks of Jesus's suffering and death as a redemptive act that happened once for all. The Bible employs many images: he bore our guilt, he paid our debt, he conquered death and evil, he gave his life for his friends, he made God present even in the abyss where we experience ourselves abandoned by God. Paul speaks of "God's foolishness": here, we encounter "what no eye has seen, nor ear heard, nor the human heart conceived" (1 Cor 2:9).

The Bible in its wisdom is aware that what happened on the cross is a divine mystery that has existed since the very beginning. The cross was indeed radically new, but not completely alien. John writes that Jesus brought us "that which was from the beginning" (John 1:1).

"Love is God's first word, the first thought that sailed across his mind," writes Knut Hamsun (in *Victoria*).[6] "When he said: 'Let there be light,' there was love. And everything that he had created was very good; and nothing thereof he wanted unmade again. And love became the origin of the world and the ruler of the world; but all love's paths are strewn with blossoms and blood, blossoms and blood."

After God had created the world, he saw that it was fertile and green and beautiful, and he saw its infinite possibilities for good and for evil. Perhaps he then lifted his hand in blessing, and made the sign of the cross upon the world. We are often told in scripture that the world was made in Christ, through Christ, and for Christ. These mysterious words must mean that in some way, the cross and the resurrection are etched onto the basic pattern of all things. And if the world bears the print of the pain *and* the reconciliation that the cross signifies, then existence as a whole is borne up by hope. There is nothing that is not—in some way or other—linked to him and marked by his sign.

When we make the sign of the cross, whether in the wings or out on the stage itself, this is not some external, alien gesture. It is a sacred act that touches our deepest nature and calls us back to what God meant us to be. When the sign of the cross is made on children's foreheads at baptism, this attests that they are to belong to the crucified and risen Jesus Christ and to believe in him who created reconciliation and life. When we follow Christ on his path to the cross, this teaches us how to find the path back to our authentic humanity.

Frøland suggests that his readers should make the sign of the cross when they sing the song "Better and Better, Day by Day," for this will put their optimism on deep foundations. If we also trained ourselves to make the sign of the cross when the harsh realities of life begin to crush us, our struggle in life would take on new dimensions.

If it is indeed true to say that the world is marked by the sign of the cross, then the innermost fibers of existence are impregnated by hope. For the cross is in harmony with life itself: pain *and* reconciliation.

To Wait—to Hope

Quite spontaneously, I accepted an invitation to give a group of pastors a lecture on "visionary preaching." A few weeks' holiday set my imagination and my capacity for wonder free to roam among more or less titanic visions of the future and of hope.

Reluctantly I was pulled back down to reality. Was it possible that the most important thing the Bible had to say about hope was an old, worn-out word—*to wait*? But I quickly discovered that it had lost nothing of its splendor. It was a golden word, completely true to reality and at the same time replete with hope.

The Bible has an extraordinary amount to say about waiting. "Israel, wait for the Lord!" People wait for the morning, or else they wait for the harvest. They wait for the day of God, for his judgment, for the light, for the time that will bring healing, for the kingdom of God, for the Messiah, for the second coming of Christ, and for the fulfillment of all things. The day is at hand. Look at the signs: the spring is coming. Keep awake and wait! Only a little while now!

Is this the word that we—modern people who find nothing positive in patience or in waiting—need to hear? We want quick solutions, speedy decisions, mobility, instant coffee, and fast food. We pare down time, we get to our destinations more quickly, we flicker from one reality to the next. We manipulate time, we eat strawberries all the year round, we fly to the southern hemisphere when it is summer there, or else we purchase the summer under a sunlamp in a studio around the corner.

In other cultures, time is the one thing they have more than enough of, because time comes as an inexhaustible gift from the future. For us, time is the one thing we do not have, because time keeps on slipping out of our grasp. It hardly seems likely that the Bible's words about "waiting" could become a vocabulary for our own hope and expectation.

But why should this be impossible? After all, we have not forgotten everything about waiting—indeed, sometimes we are forced to wait. It still takes nine months to bring a child into the world. It takes half a lifetime to become an adult, and the rest of our life is spent allowing our knowledge and experience to generate insight into life. The crises in our life take time—cares, illnesses, and dying. If love is to grow and blossom, it needs time;

the same is true of friendship, longing, and playing with our children. Sometimes we need sicknesses and crises to bring us back from all the time we have lost and to force us—against our will—to accept the gift of waiting.

If all the important things in life demand time and perseverance, there is surely all the more reason why we should wait for God. This waiting can remind us about aspects of human existence and of God that we easily overlook: God's time is not structured in keeping with our needs for quick solutions and convenient answers. It may take a whole lifetime to find the way home.

The Japanese theologian Kosuke Koyama, who spent many years in Thailand, expressed his faith in God by means of what he called "water buffalo theology."[7] He was profoundly impressed by the perennial repetitive cycles in the monsoon climate and by the slow pace of the water buffalo through the rice fields, and he realized that the eternal God does not adapt himself to Western demands for efficiency and time management. God follows the water buffalo's slow movements through history. Our efforts do not bring about his coming. Our impatient faith does not speed up his plans. But he comes.

To hope is to wait.

II

FACE TO FACE

Arise, my love, my fair one,
and come away;
for now the winter is past,
the rain is over and gone.
The flowers appear on the earth;
the time of singing has come.
(Song of Solomon 2:10–12)

We may mock Christianity,
scorn it, and find it revolting—
but the day we draw aside the veil that covers it,
we will recognize the beloved of our young days,
and our only true love.
(Jens Bjørneboe, Norwegian author)[1]

Eve, Where Are They?

One day, Eve returned to the lost garden of paradise.

She had longed and searched times without number, but the path was blocked off and the door shut. Suddenly, the Creator appeared in her wilderness—though she had not awaited him, nor even wished to meet him. Once again, her shame was laid bare; but this time, he opened up the path back to paradise.

John relates that learned and pious men had taken hold of her and set her in front of Jesus. "'Teacher,' [they said,] 'this woman was caught in the very act of committing adultery. Now in the law Moses commanded us to stone such women. Now what do you say?' They said this to test him, so that they might have some charge to bring against him" (John 8:3–11).

In Adam's company, Eve had wandered far and wide through the world. Though created in God's image, they had yielded to the temptation to believe that they could become like him, and this dream of greatness was their doom. They did not see what we have seen so clearly in the course of history—when we dare to look!—namely, that those who want to be more than a human being tend to end up something less than a human being. Adam and Eve were not able to bear the consequences of their actions, but hid from the Creator. They bowed their heads and averted their eyes.

Originally, two questions had pierced their hearts: "Adam, where are you?" and "Eve, what is this that you have done?" These questions followed them like a curse in the land east of Eden. As life became a tangled mess, they shared a common fate and sought consolation in each other—but they destroyed one another. Adam loved Eve, but his embrace could also suffocate her and crush her.

Eve loved Adam, but love was hard to bear. Was there no route back from the barren landscapes in which they now lived?

Now she meets the man who had come from God. She is not there of her own free will, but is dragged into his presence by a flock of men. The curse is still at work: Adam is both accuser and judge. He has not yet abandoned his dream of becoming like God, and now he asks God's questions: "Eve, where are you? Eve, what is this that you have done?" But he does not even wait for an answer. He knows where she has been and what she has done! He stands there, blocking the path.

Eve is held captive in a vicious circle. She has fallen victim to Adam's dream of reigning in the place of God. The men with faces of flint form a tight ring; in its center stand the woman and the new Adam, the man who came from God. She is the weapon they seek to use against him. God's law commands that such women should be stoned. What does he have to say on this question? They form an iron ring of accusers: "We have *her* already. Soon we will have *him* as well!"

Jesus breaks the circle open. He cannot stand there together with the men. He breaks ranks and stoops to write with his finger on the ground. He is aware of their eyes as they fasten on his back. He is bent down by the weight of their accusations.

The seconds tick past. What is he writing? Is he drawing Adam's face? Does he see that Adam's eye not only condemned her, but also stripped her naked? Was he aware that the men's contempt was intensified by their own lust? Did he realize that they asked God's question in order that they themselves could flee from judgment? Was he surprised that only the woman had been taken prisoner—although it is surely impossible for a woman to commit adultery all by herself? Did he see that it was Adam's world that had shaped the fate of Eve?

Now he gets up and addresses Adam: "Let anyone among you who is without sin be the first to throw a stone at her."

And here it is the Creator himself who puts the question: "Adam, where are you?" It is the merciful Lord who speaks, not in order to judge and crush, but in order to awaken—to remind the men where they were, and to call them back to reality. The words hang in the air for a little while, then the men depart quietly, the older ones first. The vicious circle of condemnation has been broken.

Once again, he stoops and writes. Is he now sketching the pattern of her life on the barren earth? Does he see the imprint of violence? Does he see eyes whose light had been extinguished, a child who never had a childhood, a woman who was never permitted to be anything other than a sex object? Is he sketching the portrait of Eve—who sinned indeed, but was just as much a victim? Is he outlining the contours of a new face, where hidden longings and shattered hopes take on a form and a life?

At last, he gets up and they stand there, face-to-face. She is no longer the sinful woman who must give an account of her misdeeds, as in the old question, "Eve, what is this that you have done?" She is a victim who has finally been freed from her oppressor and meets the gaze of the new Adam, the Son of Man and Son of God.

A new, revolutionary question is addressed to her: "Woman, where are they?" In other words: "Eve, what is this that *they* have done? Where are the men who humiliated you? And where is the man you slept with—for he too was certainly not guiltless? Where are those who condemn you?"

She can now say: "No one has condemned me!" The victim has become a human being, the vicious circle of self-contempt has been broken. For now she has met a man who did not condemn her, and this means the beginning of life: Eve has returned to the lost garden and stood face-to-face with the Creator.

Once, long ago, he had etched an image on her soul—*imago Dei*, "the image of God." Since then, that image had been soiled and was no longer clear; but no one had been able to efface it completely or tear it to pieces. Now it is summoned to life, and she glimpses a face that she had indeed forgotten, but never actually lost.

She stands up and breathes freely. Her eyes are freed from their dark clouds. The world takes on fresh color. Does she see the sprouts begin to germinate in the outlines traced by the Master on the ground? Does she notice that she is surrounded by trees and flowers and grass? Does she see that the world is new? The sun floods her with its light and shines through her broken body. Her heart beats and her blood is warm.

She stands in that first dawn when the world was created and God said: "Let there be light! Let there be life!" All is very good. Springs break forth and transform her wilderness into the Garden of Eden. The creative word has penetrated her life: "Neither do I condemn you. Go your way, and from now on do not sin again."

She straightens her back and goes out into the sunshine, a new creation lovely as a spring morning.

Do Not Stir Up Love Until It Is Ready!

The Song of Solomon is a biblical poem, beautiful and sensitive, about the love between man and woman. In every generation, it has made hearts beat more warmly, for here eyes meet, tender words are whispered, people sing and play and dance. The images are daring—they speak of longing and attraction, but also of the fear that love may die. Much is at stake:

> I adjure you, O daughters of Jerusalem,
> by the gazelles or the wild does:
> do not stir up or awaken love
> until it is ready! (Song 2:7)

For some reason, the daring images of the Song of Songs remind me of the story about Jesus and the sinful woman in the house of the pious Simon, who holds a feast for a select few, with Jesus as the guest of honor. The woman comes in from the street, stands at Jesus' feet, and weeps. Everyone knows her—she is well known in that city quarter, a notorious sinner avoided by those who were pure. An embarrassing episode! She must be removed before she destroys the good atmosphere! But the episode develops into a momentous encounter of love (Luke 7:36–49).

What is the link between the exotic and erotic images of the Song of Songs and the banquet that took a wrong turn? If we take the trouble to listen to the passion in the words Jesus speaks, we can sense that this too is a song of love. In all the drabness of a village in Galilee, with its dirt and poverty and all the dust of its gray everyday life, love breaks in—it was "awakened" when the time was ripe. Love was "stirred up" when it wanted, when it was ready to bud and blossom.

What we see in Luke's Gospel is not the playful love of two young people who exuberantly discover their feelings for one another in gardens and pavilions. There is nothing for this woman to discover: Jesus encounters someone who has plenty of experience, one who had lived by selling her body. She was broken, despised by those who made use of her sexual services, disillusioned—maybe even dirty and ugly. And now they meet one another. The one who is impure stands before the one who is pure. The time is ripe. The adventure of love between the Son of Man and a daughter of man can begin. It takes place on a different level than the romance in the Song of Songs, but it is just as passionate, just as beautiful, brimful of hope and longings.

Let us listen to her words in the Song of Songs (3:1–2, 5:7):

Upon my bed at night
I sought him whom my soul loves;
I sought him, but found him not;

I called him, but he gave no answer.
"I will rise now and go about the city,
in the streets and in the squares;
I will seek him whom my soul loves."
I sought him, but found him not…
Making their rounds in the city
the sentinels found me;
they beat me, they wounded me,
they took away my mantle,
those sentinels of the walls.

We can only guess at the desperate longing that lay hidden in the life story of the woman whom Jesus met. It is not likely that her bed was a place of rosy dreams; but she too had sought him in the streets and in the squares. She had sought eyes with light and warmth; she had waited for someone who would see more than just her body; she had dreamed of meeting a friend.

How many years had passed, while she sought but did not find? How many blows and wounds had she endured? But one day he was there. In the Song of Songs (2:4), she sings:

He brought me to the banqueting house,
and his banner over me was love.

In the Gospel story, it is Jesus who is in the banqueting house. She comes in from the street and stands at his feet. His banner over her is love.

In the poem, he entices her with his poems (Song 2:10–12):

"Arise, my love, my fair one, and come away;
for now the winter is past,
the rain is over and gone.
The flowers appear on the earth;
the time of singing has come."

"She has loved much," says Jesus of the woman. The winter is past, and she is set free to sing.

In the Song of Songs (4:9–10), he sings thus about her love:

> You have ravished my heart, my sister, my bride,
> you have ravished my heart
> with a glance of your eyes,
> with one jewel of your necklace.
> How sweet is your love, my sister, my bride!
> how much better is your love than wine,
> and the fragrance of your oils than any spice!

"Do you see this woman?" Jesus asks the pious Simon. "I entered your house; you gave me no water for my feet, but she has bathed my feet with her tears and dried them with her hair. You gave me no kiss, but from the time I came in she has not stopped kissing my feet. You did not anoint my head with oil, but she has anointed my feet with ointment" (Luke 7:44–46). These signs of her love are truly beautiful. Her love is better than wine, and the fragrance of her oils is finer than the scent of balsam. The narrator draws us into the simple drama. He paints with broad strokes and strong colors, employing familiar contrasts and tensions. The scene is the house of pious Simon, a banquet where something prevents joy from breaking out. Simon serves God with great intensity, he is irreproachable, concerned about purity, a man who awaits the new world. He has mastered life, everything is as it should be.

And yet there is something lifeless about all this. It is pale, held firmly under control, measured out. There is nothing passionate—no kiss of welcome, no touch of skin upon skin. Despite all the food and drink, the conversation falters. Here there is no laughter, no singing, no joy. On the contrary, we sense a tension in the air. The guest is being examined surreptitiously: is he truly the one he claims to be? This banquet is not a celebration of the gift of friendship, but a useful chance to put the Master to the test. Are the negative rumors true? And before anyone has a chance to formulate a verdict, these same rumors are confirmed!

She brings with her the stink of the back alleys. Her very presence is a provocation in the eyes of a man who is concerned about purity. She touches the Master and besmirches him with her tears, which she dries with her harlot's hair. She uses the language she knows best, namely body language, kisses and caresses. Jesus lets her do all this. Has he taken leave of his senses? Does he want to bring shame on the whole company?

A woman like her has no appreciation of what is appropriate in the presence of people with pure hands and a good reputation, for all that they give her are despondency and pain. In order to survive, she has shut such persons out of her life and encased herself in armor. After all, her own self-contempt is enough of a burden—she does not need to be weighed down by their condemnation too. Why should she let herself and her friends be wounded by the purity of the pious? Their pure world and her alley lie side by side, but even next-door neighbors can live in detached universes, separated by frozen light-years.

But Jesus too was pure! He too spoke about perfection! What was it she had seen in the Master with the pure heart, that the others—the pious ones—did not have? What was there in his perfection that did not wreak violence on her dignity, but instead made her heart beat more warmly?

His purity was not a protective wall. It came from within, like a bubbling spring of water. He was not afraid of being soiled by those who were impure; on the contrary, it was his purity that was contagious.

Had he passed by her as he wandered through the alleys? Had she met his eye in the crowd? Had she seen how his friendship allowed other women like herself to straighten their backs? Had the wind carried snatches of his words, so that these took root in her, as dandelion seeds cling onto barren soil? Had she seen him freely pour out his love: words about forgiveness, words against those who were hard and powerful, words about tenderness, help, consolation, hope, and expectation?

We do not know the answer to such questions; but it is certain that his purity was freely poured out. His perfection did not take God away from them: it allowed God to live in their world. "Be perfect," he had said, "as your heavenly Father is perfect." He was not speaking about irreproachable conduct and clean hands, but about the generosity of a heart that has space for everyone. "Perfection" is a whole heart that can love its enemies and bless those who curse. Look at God, and see how generous he is: "He makes his sun rise on the evil and on the good, and sends rain on the righteous and on the unrighteous" (Matt 5:43–48).

There was something that awakened her longings. The frozen springs thawed, her pain was assuaged. She stood behind Jesus and wept. Had she really preserved her generosity in the midst of her humiliation?

The narrative is not completely clear. The conversation moves on two levels, indicating that two separate motifs are being woven together here.

The clearest motif can be seen in the parable about the remission of debt: "A certain creditor had two debtors," Jesus tells Simon. "One owed five hundred denarii, and the other fifty. When they could not pay, he canceled the debts for both of them. Now which of them will love him more?" Simon answered, "I suppose the one for whom he canceled the greater debt." And Jesus said to him, "You have judged rightly" (Luke 7:41–43).

This parable expresses something we often see in the Gospels, namely the experience of being overwhelmed by boundless grace. When the terrible darkness in the woman's life story encounters the pardon Jesus gives, she responds with a passionate love. This is why Jesus says: "Her sins, which were many, have been forgiven; hence she has shown great love" (Luke 7:47).

She forms a contrast to the pious man, who does not grasp the mystery of grace because his affairs are in order. And Jesus comments, "The one to whom little is forgiven, loves little." This is the solid conviction of the Gospel, and it reveals a sure knowledge of the human heart.

At the same time, we glimpse a deeper motif. It is easy to misunderstand, and perhaps it became less clear as the story was told and retold.

One natural way to read the Greek text at Luke 7:47 is: "Her sins, which were many, have been forgiven, because she has shown great love!" This would be an echo of the discourse Jesus holds in the previous chapter of Luke, where he challenges those with narrow, stingy hearts and says that the one who gives generously will receive a generous reward: "A good measure, pressed down, shaken together, running over, will be put into your lap; for the measure you give will be the measure you get back" (Luke 6:38).

Some interpreters think they are being daring and provocative when they suggest that since the prostitute had made love very often, and had in fact earned her living by doing so, she was worthy of God's love. But it is presumably only men who can reflect in such a superficial manner on the activity of buying and selling sex, which destroys true humanity and oppresses women. There is nothing in the words or actions of Jesus to indicate that he romanticizes the sinful brutality that turns a woman's body, and love itself, into an object of merchandise.

He is speaking of a love that lies deeper. His words, "She has shown great love," reveal that the way she approached him has reminded him somehow of his own perfection. She has a generosity of spirit that is open to God's generous presence, and she has a whole heart that responds with utter love.

Once again, we see the contrast between Simon and the prostitute. He is a believer; his prayers and his profession of faith are correct, and God is the center of his life. He is a God-fearing man, and yet his heart is too narrow. What about her? Can we really believe that there was any place for God in her struggle for survival? She scarcely understood the prayers of the pious; their words about "responsibility" and "calling" were an affront to her, because they reeked of oppression and of interference in her life. Nevertheless, it was she who recognized the presence of love. Love was awakened when it was ready, and she responded by loving him with all her heart and all her soul and all her strength.

Perhaps we see something of the generosity of the woman's humanity when the language she had used in the days of her degradation—tears, body language, passion, kisses, caresses—is redeemed as she turns to Jesus in love.

Was her weeping the turning point, the symbol of a spring of water that is released and begins to flow? Tears can mean many things: bitterness, cares, powerlessness, despair over lost chances, repentance and penance, overwhelming joy, and love. And nothing is worse than a shuttered heart: frozen bitterness, paralyzed care, resigned despair, a rebellion that is crushed. In this woman's tears, the springs of water are released. Care and bitterness and repentance join hands with expectancy and exultation over the life that is breaking forth. Love is awakened.

It is not true to claim that love makes us blind. It is love that gives us eyes to see. A generous heart sees God when he shows himself, but a narrow heart—no matter how pious it may be—has no place for him. The pious man remains solitary in his pure world, while the impure woman with the generous heart is transformed by love.

"Your faith has saved you," says Jesus. "Go in peace" (Luke 7:50).

> "Arise, my love,
> For now the winter is past…
> The flowers appear on the earth;
> the time of singing has come." (Song 2:10–12)

Where did she go? What songs did she sing? Luke goes on to tell us that many women followed Jesus, so perhaps she joined them. Perhaps she learned something other than body language. Perhaps she received words and prayers, so that she could sing a new song. I picture her, hearing and repeating for the first time the words in David's Psalm that so many other dejected and thankful people had used in the centuries before her (Ps 30:1, 5, 11–12):

> I will extol you, O LORD,
> for you have drawn me up…
> For his anger is but for a moment;
> his favor is for a lifetime.
> Weeping may linger for the night,
> but joy comes with the morning…
> You have turned my mourning into dancing;
> you have taken off my sackcloth
> and clothed me with joy,
> so that my soul may praise you and not be silent.
> O LORD my God, I will give thanks to you forever.

With Hope as Guest

During a conference about "the anatomy of hatred" in 1990, Vaclav Havel, first President of the Czech Republic, spoke about hope. The simple words of this poet and statesman gave hope a profounder dimension:

> I am not an optimist, because I do not know if things will go well. Nor am I a pessimist, because I do not know if things will go badly. All I can have is hope. Hope does not depend on the specific situation. It has nothing to do with external circumstances. Hope is something you have—or do not have. I thank God for this gift.[2]

This is not so far removed from Paul's description of Abraham, our father in faith, in the Letter to the Romans: "Hoping against hope, he believed" (Rom 4:18). In a later chapter he paints a dramatic picture of the pain of the world. "The whole creation has been groaning in labor pains until now; and not only the creation, but we ourselves sigh and groan" (Rom 8:22–23). We are not even able to formulate meaningful prayers. Everything is subject to transience. And yet, there is hope!

In the Bible, hope is not based on optimistic or pessimistic calculations. Hope is a profession of faith. Hope is faith's defiance of circumstances. When one who despairs sings her lamentation, it is not in order to communicate her pessimism, but to remind God that he has promised to be faithful.

We find one of the most beautiful and deeply moving songs of hope precisely in the lamentation uttered by a man whose life was shattered (Lam 3:1–30). He was familiar with captivity and hunger, isolation and bitterness, contempt and loss of honor. Patiently, he had borne the yoke in his youth. Now he sits alone and is silent, he bends down with his mouth to the dust. He turns his cheek to the one who strikes him, and is filled with disgrace. Nevertheless, he says: "There may yet be hope! The Lord is my portion, therefore I will hope in him." He speaks on behalf of millions of wretched people who may have little reason to hope, but defiantly proclaim: "There may yet be hope!"

And now we hear the voices of some women, for they too know something about hope. A woman who had been cast out—Hagar, Abraham's servant maid and the mother of his child—asked in the depths of her distress: "Have I really seen a glimpse of him who sees me?" A jealous mistress had driven her away, and she searched despairingly for water for herself and her child. When an angel showed her a spring in the wilderness, she formulated one of the earliest names given to God in the Bible: "You are a God who sees." And she called the spring "Well of the Living One who sees me" (Gen 16:13–14).

"A God who sees"—we encounter this profession of faith throughout the entire Bible, in a thousand variations. God is the defender of widows and father of orphans, the one who is on the side of foreigners and the poor. These were the societal groups most at risk, people who had lost every source of security, the first to suffer from injustice. Who would protect them from violence? A golden thread running through the whole Bible proclaims that God has a special care for these rejected persons. He is "the Living One who sees."

On any human calculation, the most realistic reaction of all these little ones to their situation would be despair. Is not the song of lamentation right to say (Ps 94:5–7):

> [The evildoers] crush your people, O LORD,
> and afflict your heritage.
> They kill the widow and the stranger,
> they murder the orphan,
> and they say, "The LORD does not see;
> the God of Jacob does not perceive."

And was not Job right to complain about God's inaccessibility (Job 9:11, 16, 18):

> Look, he passes by me, and I do not see him;
> he moves on, but I do not perceive him…
> If I summoned him and he answered me,
> I do not believe that he would listen to my voice…
> He will not let me get my breath,
> but fills me with bitterness.

There is almost something shocking about the honesty with which the Bible confronts the realities of life: fear is not camouflaged, qualms and doubts are not expelled into that dark borderland where unbelief and denial make their conquests. On the contrary, all this is taken into the sphere of faith, as lamentation and accusation hurled against the Most High, as protest, as a defiant profession of faith in the One who had promised to be faithful. The human person does not simply accept his lot in life! No, he says: "The Lord is my portion, therefore I will hope in him." The one who believes, straightens his back and waits (Lam 3:49–50):

> My eyes will flow without ceasing,
> without respite,
> until the LORD from heaven
> looks down and sees.

This perspective is deepened by an episode in the Gospel. Luke relates that Jesus, on his wanderings through Galilee, met a funeral cortege outside the town of Nain. "A man who had died was being carried out. He was his mother's only son, and she was a widow; and with her was a large crowd from the town. When the Lord saw her, he had compassion for her and said to her, 'Do not weep.' Then he came forward and touched the bier, and the bearers stood still. And he said, 'Young man, I say to you, rise!' The dead man sat up and began to speak, and Jesus gave him to his mother. Fear seized all of them; and they glorified God, saying, 'A great prophet has risen among us!' and 'God has visited his people'" (Luke 7:11–17).

The widow had lost the hope on which she had relied for her old age. She had lost literally everything, for her son was her only "life insurance." Now she was on her way out of the town—out of human fellowship. The crowd took part in her mourning, no doubt, as people did at that time, with wailing music, lamentation, and weeping. Her neighbors would sympathize with her for a while, but in the long run they would have more than enough to do with their own needs. Where could she find any hope? Must not she too think: "The Lord does not see; the God of Jacob does not perceive"?

But her despondency does not have the last word. We do not know whether the embers of a faith in "the Living One who sees" still glowed beneath her bitter lamentation; but the narrative flames up in a gloriously bright profession of hope.

First comes consolation. When Jesus saw the widow, "he had compassion for her and said to her, 'Do not weep.'" The God who sees is a God who consoles. And then comes the miracle. "He came forward and touched the bier," raised up the young man, "and gave him to his mother."

The loud music dies away, the cries of the wailing women peter out. The din gives way to calm. In their confusion, the people of Nain have no idea of what is going on; yet in the space of a few silent seconds—which must have seemed an eternity—they stand face-to-face with "the Living One who sees."

And then the din breaks out afresh, in amazement and terror. What is happening? They have recourse to history, in order to interpret what has just happened, crying out: "A great prophet has risen among us! God has visited his people!" They knew that a prophet did not speak in his own name, but in the name of God. The words Jesus addressed to the dead man were God's own creative words: "Thus says the Lord: Be alive!" When the creative word rings out, it is God who is visiting his people.

The unknown guest gives the widow back her future. He tears away the veil of grief and wipes her tears, so that her pale cheeks glow anew with color. Then he leads the crowd in through the town gate—back to human fellowship, back to life. The musicians fumble for the appropriate notes: who can cope with reversals as abrupt as this? But when God visits his people, they must celebrate, and so the joyful feast begins. Jesus and the widow lead the dance, which quickly widens to become a whirling circle in which all take part—the rich and the poor, the well dressed and the shabby. Nothing else is fitting when the Most High visits the earth.

The word translated here "visit" means literally "to look after." The God who sees does not look at the world with a passive feeling of compassion: he looks after his people. The word has many nuances: it means both to help and to visit. "I was sick and you looked after me," says Jesus in one of his great discourses about our responsibility for the weak (Matt 25:36), and James writes that true worship consists in looking after widows and orphans in their distress (Jas 1:27).

The widow had been en route to the wilderness that was her fate, and she too could have uttered Hagar's amazed question: "Have I really seen a glimpse of him who sees me?" The one who sees led her back to the land of the living, and the crowd left their cries of lamentation to shout in exultation: "God has visited his people!"

Is there any real hope for us in all of this? Is not this narrative rather a weak consolation for us who live today, two thousand years later?

Actually, we might also ask: Was it a consolation then? If it really did happen, was it anything more than one isolated incident of fulfilled hope? What about the widows in the neighboring village? Or what about the poor people who still sat in their wretchedness outside the town gate? And the widow's son died a second time, later on. No one could guarantee that their cares and misery would not become even more bitter. Can we hold fast to hope in a world so illimitably full of misery and injustice—the world we see everyday flickering across our television screens? Can the story of a God who sees and who visits the earth make us straighten our backs in hope?

The Bible's "hope" is not a vision of the world through rose-tinted glasses. Faith's expectation is not built on pious distortions of reality. We can no longer believe in the old illusions about a world that is completely beautiful and well ordered. We are indeed told that God at the beginning looked on his work and saw that it was very good (Gen 1:31), but the creation is ambiguous, as we have already seen in Paul's vision of its pains, like the throes and groans of a woman giving birth (Rom 8:22). Wickedness and transitoriness are part of reality.

The One who saw that the creation was good continued to see. His eyes darkened and his face blanched when he saw evil and violence invade the earth. He saw rebellion. He saw brother murder brother. He saw hatred. Was there no longer any place for him? Was the world slipping out of his hands? Was he to become a foreigner in the universe he himself had shaped, a guest in his own house?

The Bible expresses this in a picture: God no longer walked with human beings in the garden. They failed to carry out the task assigned them, and forgot God. But he did not forget his earth. He continued to see, and his eyes were filled with compassion. Again and again he visited his people. John writes that Christ "came to what was his own, and his own people did not accept him" (John 1:11). But he did also find some who received him and recognized him. Every time God visited the earth, every time he was seen, something happened to those who received him. They stood upright and glimpsed the outlines of a new world. Their hope glowed brightly.

Perhaps the word *visit* can give us the key to understand the narratives in the Gospels. It has a transient ring to it: a guest arrives and then departs after a few hours' visit. There is something similarly transient about the stories of Jesus—they are fragments in a mighty drama, or glimpses of a greater whole. Brief episodes are strung together, often with no clear links: events, conversations, banquets, healings, discourses, discussions, parables, and finally the great drama of his suffering and death and resurrection.

All these narratives are chunks of life, rapid, transient. At the same time, each "chunk" is intensely full of a meaning that is grasped by those who see and hear. The guest arrives and departs, but life is different once he has been with us.

This transience characterizes Jesus's life as a whole. We know virtually nothing about the first thirty years. Then we have one year—or perhaps three—full of intense activity, before death and judgment overtake him. Perhaps it is not by chance that he himself likens his presence to a banquet; he asks: "The wedding guests cannot fast while the bridegroom is with them, can they?" (Mark 2:19). Now is the time of rejoicing, so let us celebrate God's feast! God is close at hand, God has become accessible. We can discern his face clearly. His world takes on form and color.

"The kingdom of God is among you," said Jesus (Luke 17:21). See it! Enter it! And they did indeed see how things changed in his presence. Then he was gone...God had visited the earth.

Only a glimpse? Yes. A fleeting guest? Yes, indeed. But at the same time, the narratives retain their validity as glorious promises about a God who sees, a God who visits the earth and is close to everyone who recognizes him and opens the door to him.

And have we not seen at least a glimpse of this? It is clearest in some of the great women and men of the church, whose lives made God visible, famous and unknown believers who transmitted the radiance of the light shed by God's presence; innumerable men and women who defied every reversal of fortune in order to live their lives for others; those who were willing to sacrifice life and limb under brutal regimes in order to oppose injustice. But we see this in our own little world too: the woman who goes to her neighbor and asks forgiveness; the married couple who find the way back to their first love; sick and lonely and broken persons who are restored to fellowship and joy by the care and prayer of others. "I was sick and you took care of me; I was in prison and you visited me" (Matt 25:36). Those who "look after widows and orphans" and other deprived persons in today's society not only take part in the true worship, as James (1:27) says; they are also doing God's own deeds. They share in the feast when God visits his people.

When this happens, the world takes on a more authentic form. We return to what God meant us to be and sense what he had in mind at the beginning, when he saw that everything was very good. Then God's world is no longer a dream about something that lies only beyond death: it takes on shape and color in human beings who meet one another, with faces and bodies, in words and looks and embraces. In a glimpse, we anticipate the world, which at present is accessible to us only in images and signs, but which will become a reality when God completes his work.

This brings us to our conclusion, the great vision of hope. We await a fulfillment, when God—and with him, hope—is no longer a transient guest, but dwells among us. Whatever we say about this hope goes far beyond our human ideas, for we simply do not know enough. Nevertheless, we need not be silent, because we do know *something* about it, thanks to the rich imagery of the Bible, which speaks of a hope anticipated in glimpses of God's presence, not least when we are told about the God who visits the earth. In the visions of a new heaven and the new earth in the Book of Revelation, God is no mere transient guest: "See, the home of God is among mortals. He will dwell with them as their God; they will be his people, and God himself will be with them" (Rev 21:3).

In the Gospel, we see how Jesus is moved to compassion for the widow. He consoles her, he makes her weeping cease, and he leads her back to life. Surely we see a reflection of such wonderful experiences in the description of the fulfillment of all things in the Book of Revelation: "He will wipe every tear from their eyes. Death will be no more; mourning and crying and pain will be no more, for the first things have passed away" (Rev 21:4).

Jesus lived among people who were oppressed, despised, and pushed aside. The Book of Revelation was written for a church that was on the point of being wiped out by persecutions. But at the same time, they had a hope that God would bring all things to fulfillment, a hope born of the ancient profession of faith in a God who sees, a hope confirmed by Jesus, in whose life God visited the earth.

Hope does not depend on the specific situation, Vaclav Havel said. Hope does not depend on external circumstances. It is something one either has or does not have. I thank God for this gift.

The Mystery of John's Name

The church's calendar celebrates two births, one in midsummer and one in midwinter. John the Baptist belongs to the summer, but a shadow lies over his face; Jesus is celebrated in midwinter, but he brings with him the light of the coming sun.

John's feast is June 24, when the days are long and the sun is high in the heavens. John's task was to prepare the way for the Lord in the wilderness. He was the fiery prophet of the new age, speaking under a burning sun and almost consumed by the glowing heat of faith. He exhorted people to perform works of penance, to prepare for the coming of him who was greatest of all. All the time, he pointed forward to another: "He must increase, but I must decrease" (John 3:30). After his feast day, the sun declines in strength. As the year marches on, St. John's light grows dim.

For people in earlier times, the symbolism of the seasons intensified the drama in the story. The days grow paler as we draw nearer to the dark months of the year; the sun loses its strength, the fire sinks down.

Now we meet John at the very end of his path, rotting away in a prison. Has he decreased even further than he had foreseen? When he was flooded by the sun's rays, he had seen everything so clearly. Now the light disappears, and his senses are filled by darkness. It will soon be midwinter.

Finally, the one who was to increase speaks about the one who is decreasing. The new sun sheds his radiance on the Baptist's darkness: "Among those born of women no one has arisen greater than John the Baptist," says Jesus. John is the last of the great series of men of God who prepared God's kingdom. "For all the prophets and the law prophesied until John came; and if you are willing to accept it, he is Elijah who is to come. Let anyone with ears listen!" (Matt 11:11–15).

＞ ＜

The Gospels never separate Jesus and John; nor does the church do so. What about us?

Jesus and John are present, of course—they have their place in our dogmatic systems and in the scriptural texts we read in church. But they are not unproblematic, because they both confront us with intolerable demands. They resist our efforts to restrain them in the niches in which we would like to keep them. If only they could have been a little less one-sided!

Jesus knew people's hearts, and he compares them to children who refuse to join in a game:

> We played the flute for you, and you did not dance;
> we wailed, and you did not mourn. (Matt 11:17)

When the suggestion is made that they "play weddings" with dancing and feasting, they refuse to join in—and they react in the same way when the suggestion is made that they "play funerals" with weeping and wailing. Here, Jesus sums up what has happened to himself and to John. John brought a message of repentance and fasting. When people saw that he "neither ate nor drank," they called him a fanatic and said, "He has a demon!"; but it was just as bad when the Son of Man came and celebrated life with eating and drinking, for then they said, "Look, a glutton and a drunkard, a friend of tax collectors and sinners!" (Matt 11:16–19).

Both John and Jesus presented the crowds with a challenge. They attracted many people and opened their eyes to see what a new life could look like. But then their demands went beyond all proportions, and they had to be shown who was in charge: John was removed by an evil king; Jesus fell victim to the men who held religious and political power.

We have other methods to neutralize them today. We try to make them fit our own ideas, making their words nicer here, reinterpreting them a little there, or smoothing out the rough edges. We domesticate them and hush up their exaggerations, so that they fit neatly into our own small lives.

We dismiss John quickly, drawing his sting by means of a theology that allocates him to the "old covenant." For does not Jesus himself draw a clear demarcating line between the time that led up to John, and the new age that begins with Christ? So we say that John represents the law; he did not yet know the Gospel of grace. Or else we appeal to our feelings—surely we have enough prophets of gloom as it is? Why should we supply fuel to our despondent mood by drawing on the bleak gloom of the Baptist's pessimism? Was he not merely a man who hated life, one who tortured himself and other people out there in the wilderness? Did he not reject the world? And did he not infect other spiritual refugees with his own darkness?

John was certainly a severe man. But the flame in his spirit was fed by God's own burning anger at injustice and violence, and here John is completely at one with the ancient prophets of Israel. Indeed, the same flame sometimes flared up in Jesus' preaching too. John may seem gloomy, but he was in fact holding up a lamp that allowed his contemporaries to see. The chief aim of his words was not to condemn, but to cry out that God was coming to right wrongs and to bring the world back to its original form. His aim was to "make the wilderness like Eden" and "the desert like the garden of the LORD," as an ancient prophecy had foretold (Isa 51:3).

The Baptist's name contains a great mystery. *John* means "God is gracious." John's words seek to create life. His message means transformation.

Once, when I was a child, we were playing on a sunny beach. At the meeting point between sand and woodland, I found a big sheet of corrugated iron that set my imagination working. Did it conceal unknown treasures? I got a terrific shock when I used all my strength to heave it up and saw all the little snakes wriggling there in the darkness. That is exactly what John the Baptist did. He peeled away the façade of prettiness and pretense and ambitions, and the snakes wriggled out into the sunlight. He was shocked and cried out: "You brood of vipers! Who warned you to flee from the wrath to come?" (Matt 3:7).

Most of us want to avoid anything that smacks of penance. We want things to get better—for ourselves, for our marriage partner, for our families—and we dream of change and of life. We want a world that is more just, an end to injustice and oppression! We want a life that is more whole and fuller, maybe even a life that is more honest. But we know, deep down, that change and new life are impossible without pain, penance, and difficult choices. If life is to be different, something must be given up.

It is difficult to talk about penance to people who grew up in a strict Christian environment, for some heard so much about penance that their lives were crushed and broken. Their problems stem from a pattern drummed into them by preachers and youth leaders who talked incessantly about sin and grace—and about little else!—invading the hidden chambers of their souls and wielding power over them by means of the guilt feelings they kindled. In this system, penance was a preprogrammed emotional pattern that led, surely and repeatedly, from distress at one's sin to joy on hearing the proclamation of grace.

One of the first passages in the Bible that I myself underlined with red ink was Paul's words: "But where sin increased, grace abounded all the more" (Rom 5:20); I was fourteen at the time. This is a liberating message, but it is easy to twist it around. Penance became an experience of being sinful and small, and the feeling that one was a failure had to be intensified in order to intensify the message about forgiveness. We got stuck in an experience that all too easily puts down profound roots in us, namely: "I am not good enough, I cannot change myself, I am not making any progress." This leads us to cling desperately onto grace, instead of allowing grace to penetrate us and create new life in us.

The Baptist did not intend to make people *feel* that they were sinful. Penance was not a feeling of silent pain while one waited to hear the assurance of God's grace. No, John wanted people to *act*. He wanted to see a change. The people who came to him said: "What shall we do?" and John demanded a change that hurt: "Whoever has two coats must share with anyone who has none; and whoever has food must do likewise." He deprived the tax collectors and the soldiers of their most cherished privileges when he told the tax collectors: "Collect no more than the amount prescribed for you," and the soldiers: "Do not extort money from anyone by threats" (Luke 3:10–20). He also reprimanded the king for his wicked deeds.

If John is indeed the one who prepares the way for Christ, we cannot separate these two figures. Both are sent by the gracious and merciful Creator, who wants to see life and change; and both spoke of the new kingdom of God.

John lived in his own landscape, a barren wilderness far from human society. People had to go out to him in order to do penance. And some saw how the wilderness was transformed into a flowering garden.

Jesus's landscape was the villages and town squares of Galilee, where people lived in a dirt and stench and poverty that anyone who has been in the Near East can easily picture. Their world was unjust, with a few rich people living at the cost of mass poverty; sickness was very common, with skin rashes, scabies, and itches, with backs bent double by heavy burdens, with aching hands and painful wounds. Here, there were children and old people, fishermen, farmers, peddlers, and officials; women who were exhausted almost before their lives had begun; and there were despised persons who were thought to be outside God's protection: lepers, those possessed by demons, street girls, collaborators with the Roman occupation, the dregs of society.

This is Jesus's landscape. He stands in the midst of this swarming life and proclaims that the wedding feast is now beginning. Do you not see that the bridegroom has come to meet his bride? Do you not hear the music? Do you not see that joy is not something we "possess," but something that comes into being wherever people reach out to one another? Jesus touched the vulnerable core of people's destinies. He entered their lives and promised them eternal fidelity. He wanted to love and honor them and remain with them in good days and bad, until...no, not "until death should part them," but even through death and the grave. He spoke about God—indeed, he lived God—in such a way that they saw God vividly before them. A new world took shape. He laughed and danced with the young people at the feast, and they received dreams and hopes for the future. He blessed the children and declared that they were the principal guests. The women breathed more freely and began to bloom. The sick and the lame felt that life was returning to them. Those who had become accustomed to hiding away in alleys to sell what people called "love" were drawn to the warmth, and they discovered that love is not an item of merchandise, but can only be received and given.

Was it strange that they poured out their tears and love on him? The warmth and light from the feast filtered out to the tax collectors—cheats who acquired power in society with the help of the foreign occupying power—and even their hard hearts began to beat anew, their cheeks began to glow, and a light was kindled in their eyes. Nothing like this had ever been seen before. Could Jesus be the one who was to come?

But now the mood in the crowd shifts to unease. Some of the guests begin to think how late it is getting—they wait for a sign that allows them to leave. Their lips are pursed, their foreheads furrowed. People start whispering in the corners. Is the feast going on too long? Is the joy beginning to wear off? Or is the opposite true—is there too much of a good thing, with far too many people being admitted to the feast and too much of a din? Ought there not to be clear rules about who can take part? The forgiveness of sins may be a good thing, but there has to be a limit somewhere!

How strange: goodness is too much for people to cope with. Those whose affairs are in order begin to leave. They are afraid that Jesus's actions may set a new pattern. Forgiveness is far too demanding. Jesus makes God come alive for them, but they do not feel safe with this God: is God no longer on the side of those who are good? Ought not God to support respectable people in their work for the good of society?

Suddenly, Jesus's message about the forgiveness of sins is an ever greater problem than John's sermons about penance. Perhaps it is easier to accept penance and judgment, for that keeps things in their proper place! But Jesus's message simply goes too far. What are they to make of his blasphemous affirmations about a God who visits those whose own actions have put them outside the pale?

They might perhaps have managed to tolerate such sinners —if only they had kept their sins a secret in their dank back alleys, and not burst out into the open, where they embarrassed respectable persons. They might have accepted that whatever the sinners had done now genuinely belonged to the past; perhaps, in the last analysis, the sinners were only unfortunate. They may be filthy dogs, but perhaps they can still do some useful work. But no one can seriously propose that such persons should receive a share in the future—that the sinners should take part in the great feast alongside Abraham, Isaac, and Jacob; that they should dance with the sons and daughters of the respectable persons; that the respectable should look them in the face without disdain and say, "You are my brother, you are my sister"! For that would mean dragging God into the mud.

And so, most of the guests withdrew. Yet more and more people came to the feast, people who longed for the bridegroom. They knocked at the door, to get a taste of joy. And they were caught up in something that transformed their entire existence. They no longer had any reason to curse their lives, for now—perhaps for the first time—they understood what blessing was.

Somewhere out in the darkness, the Baptist sits and tries to keep up with what is happening. He has heard rumors, and sometimes the music and noise from the feast seep into his dingy cell. A ray from the dawning day chases away the shadow from his gloom. He shakes his head and tries to conceal a smile. It seems that joy is taking hold of him, and those who listen hard may perhaps hear him murmur: "Was this what you meant, Lord? Now at last I am beginning to understand why you gave me the name John: 'God is gracious'!"

A God Who Lets Himself Be Mocked: Islam and Ourselves

Many years ago, Kenneth Cragg's book *Sandals at the Mosque*[3] gave new impulses to my thoughts and feelings. The author was a missionary and researcher of Islam. In this book, he sums up his decades-long experience of meeting Islam and formulates his vision of a meaningful interreligious encounter. The Bible tells us that Moses took off his shoes before the burning bush because he stood on holy ground. In the same way, says Cragg, we must take off our sandals outside the mosque. With deep reverence, we must follow Muslims into their own world. We must listen, see, and learn. We must hear the meaning that lies behind the words and grasp the life that lies behind the external forms. Perhaps this will allow us to meet one another in a profound dialogue.

When Cragg wrote his book, he took it for granted that such a dialogue would take place somewhere in the Near East, Northern Africa, or Pakistan. Forty years later, we could equally well locate it in one of our own big cities, since the religious map of Europe is undergoing immense transformations. Oslo, the capital of Norway, has many mosques; 25 percent of its school-children have a foreign language as their mother tongue, and most of these come from Islamic cultures. They are clearly visible on the streets of the city because of their skin color. But many have taken Norwegian citizenship, and even more wish to do so.

Some Norwegians follow them into their worlds, working side by side with them. They are angered by racism and discrimination. Sometimes they are disturbed by customs they do not completely understand or accept. And some follow them into their sanctuaries.

Although the traditional faith and morality of the Christian church is much closer to Muslims than many of the values that now set the tone in Norwegian society, it is not easy for them to step over the threshold of a church building, and few do so. If they come, they are welcome as our guests, since we are brothers and sisters who share at least some of the same inheritance. There ought to be a place in our sanctuary for their presence, their prayers, and their devotion.

But do we believe in the same God?

Simple answers to this question are unsatisfactory; it may be that the question itself is formulated wrongly. But if an answer is required, we must first say a crystal-clear yes, and then an equally crystal-clear no.

Respect for Islam and for Muslims' devotion requires us to affirm that they are seeking God, that they bow down before the one Lord, and that he hears their prayers. The Book of Psalms says: "He who planted the ear, does he not hear?" (Ps 94:9). Muslims' profession of faith in the one Lord, merciful and gracious, the Lord over the day of judgment, is a true profession that is confirmed by the deepest instincts in our own faith.

Respect for our own faith requires us to affirm that God rejoices in every Muslim who bows down humbly with his forehead to the ground and submits to the Lord of the world.

At the same time, respect for Islam and for its devotion requires us to affirm that we do not believe in the same God. Islam rejects some of the central insights in the Christian faith, namely the profession of faith in the Father, the Son, and the Holy Spirit, one God in three Persons, and the confession that Christ is the Son of God, true God and true man. A Muslim who converts to Christianity does more than abandon a few dogmatic propositions in exchange for new ones: he has fallen away from the faith, he has betrayed his religion, and in some countries he can be condemned to death.

Equally, respect for our own faith forbids us to affirm that we believe in the same God. Islam and Christianity do indeed both profess that God is one, but the very heart of the Muslim profession is shattered by the Christian belief in God—for we believe in a God who is *God in Christ*. Our profession that Jesus Christ is true God and true man is blasphemy in a Muslim's ears.

At the outset of our reflections, it is important to underline the closeness and the fellowship in our faith in the one God.

Jews, Christians, and Muslims are aware of sharing a common inheritance. We are all children of Abraham. Jews and Christians speak of "the God of Abraham, Isaac, and Jacob," while Muslims trace their descent back to Abraham and Ishmael.

Ishmael was Abraham's son by Hagar, the servant maid. The Book of Genesis relates how she was driven out into the wilderness and was on the point of dying when at last she found water and gave God the name: "You are a God who sees" (Gen 16:13). Although the Koran relates the story differently, it contains many of the same elements.

Pilgrims in Mecca today still take part in rites that reflect Hagar's desperate search for a spring of water in the wilderness. Indeed, the pilgrimage as a whole is full of allusions to Abraham, Hagar, and Ishmael. The pilgrims go around the Ka'ba seven times in the direction of the sun, as (according to Islam) Abraham himself did. They run back and forth seven times in the streets of Mecca, in memory of Hagar's desperate search for water in the desert. At the Zamzam spring, very close to the Ka'ba, they draw water from the spring that the angel Gabriel caused to break forth. The climax comes from the eighth day onward, with a three-day journey to various places outside Mecca. The pilgrims stand in the burning sun for half a day in memory of Abraham who "stood" against the idols; they throw stones in memory of Abraham's fight with the devil; and they conclude with a sacrifice that recalls Abraham's sacrifice. This is one of Islam's two annual feasts, and Muslims all over the world join in celebrating it.

The brothers Isaac and Ishmael did not have a particularly good relationship, but both had Abraham as their father. We call him "our father in faith," since he "hoped against hope" and believed in God's promise. Muslims look on him as the first Muslim, because he destroyed the idols and sought the one Lord. The word Islam means "subjection," and a Muslim is one who "subjects himself" in devotion to the one Lord. Because Abraham sought God and was devoted to him, the Koran affirms that he too was a Muslim (Sura 1:125f.):

> When his Lord said to him: "Devote yourself to me,"
> he replied, "I devote myself to the Lord of all the world."
> And Abraham enjoined this upon his sons and Jacob:
> "My sons, God has chosen the religion for you,
> so do not die other than serving in devotion."

Islam is "serving" Allah, the Lord of all the world, merciful and gracious, the Lord over the day of judgment, "in devotion" (Sura 1:1).

We also know that Islam counts the biblical prophets, from Adam to Christ, as its own. Muslims accord Jews and Christians a special status as "people of the Book." They speak of the Gospel (*injil*), venerate Mary as the mother of Jesus, affirm the virginal birth, and relate Jesus's miracles. Although there is much else that divides us, let us not forget that we also have a common patrimony.

Perhaps we can sum this up in the words of the Second Vatican Council, in its "Declaration on Non-Christian Religions" (1965), which exhorts the churches to look on the Muslims with respect, since "they worship God, who is one, living and subsistent, merciful and almighty, the Creator of heaven and earth, who has also spoken to humanity." Their fear of God, the place prayer has in their life, and their moral ideals demand our respect. Despite centuries of mutual strife and enmity, the Council "now pleads with all to forget the past, and urges that a sincere effort be made to achieve mutual understanding; for the benefit of all, let them together preserve and promote peace, liberty, social justice, and moral values." This exhortation should not be forgotten.

The period in the Christian yearly cycle that particularly underlines the contrast between Christianity and Islam is Lent and Eastertide. The Christian fast is a preparation for the great paschal drama. The entire Christian church turns toward Jerusalem and follows Jesus on his path to suffering and death.

Jesus's life had reached a turning point. His activity in Galilee was drawing to a close, and he had begun to make it clear to his disciples that he must go to Jerusalem and suffer greatly: he would be killed, but would rise again on the third day. This was not something they wanted to hear, and their spokesman, Peter, took Jesus aside and began to reprimand him: "God forbid it, Lord! This must never happen to you." But Jesus turned and said to Peter, "Get behind me, Satan! You are a stumbling block to me; for you are setting your mind not on divine things, but on human things" (Matt 16:21–23).

It is not by chance that Lent begins in my church precisely with this narrative. Jesus rejects Peter's spontaneous protest against suffering and death as a satanic temptation. Peter's objection shows that he has no appreciation of the deepest divine mystery. In the background, we hear the words from the Letter to the Hebrews about the Master who learned mercy by becoming like his brothers and sisters and "being tested in every respect as we are" (Heb 4:15). The hymns we sing during Lent dwell on the path Jesus took toward suffering and summon us to follow him on this path. One Scandinavian hymn puts it like this:

> See, we are going up to Jerusalem
> in the holy Lenten season.
> We see where Jesus, God's own Son,
> suffers in place of sinners.

Jerusalem is a holy city for Jews, Christians, and Muslims. Here the three religions meet; but this is also a city split apart by the three. For the Jews, it is Zion, the beautiful city, the center of God's promises and of human longings, the holy place with its temple and worship and traditions. For Muslims too, this is a holy city, woven into the accounts of the revelations to the Prophet, and the Al-Aqsa mosque on the temple square is one of Islam's central sanctuaries (Sura 17:1). For Christians, it is also the place where Jesus was humbled most deeply.

Jerusalem is a common patrimony that divides us—not only in the political sphere, but in the living heart of faith.

Let us take off our sandals in front of the city gates. Let us go in together and walk side by side, listening and speaking quiet words.

Here is my part in the conversation, based on texts that contradict the narratives in the Koran. For a Christian, these are indispensable insights into the presence of the One who is holy, insights elaborated in the simple story of the Master who showed us God's path as he made his way toward Jerusalem.

I have already mentioned that Islam respects Jesus: he is Messiah, prophet, bearer of a message, God's servant, the word that comes from God. But the contradiction becomes virtually intolerable when we speak of his cross and death: whereas we profess that he "suffered under Pontius Pilate, was crucified, died and was buried, and descended into the realm of the dead," it seems that the Koran rejects the claim that Jesus genuinely died on the cross. Sura 4:156 affirms that, while the Jews believed they had killed the Messiah, Jesus the son of Mary, God's messenger,

> They did not kill him, nor did they crucify him,
> but that was how things looked to them…
> On the contrary, God took him to himself.
> God is powerful and wise.

These words are not completely clear, but according to Islamic tradition, God liberated Jesus from the cross and "took him to himself."

Kenneth Cragg, who left his sandals outside the mosque in order to be present in the Muslim world, emphasizes that for Islam, the point was the profession of faith that the crucifixion ought not to have happened. Love could not be conquered like this! And that is why Islam seeks to "rescue" Jesus from dying on the cross. In a way, they agree with Peter in his protest against the unreasonableness of Jesus's fate.[4]

For the church, however, this is a question of life or death. It involves more than just fidelity to the events that actually occurred in that place and time; our image of God is at stake here. At this point, it is easy for the conversation to become dead-locked, so we must choose our words with care when we speak clearly about something so essential to us.

A number of years ago, a lacerating conflict about blasphemy broke out after Muslims across the world felt that a book by Salman Rushdie soiled the Prophet and his message, and hence mocked their God. In the same way, Christians have often felt grief and anger when it seems that their faith is being made the object of ridicule. We have often reacted by quoting the words of scripture: "God is not mocked" (Gal 6:7). Our Muslim friends would put it even more strongly, affirming that God is the exalted One, the almighty, utterly removed from all weakness. His name is holy, and must not be besmirched. All mockery must be punished, all resistance must be overcome.

Nevertheless, the Gospel surely says exactly the opposite! If Jesus is truly the face and the presence of God in the world, then we believe de facto in a God who lets himself be mocked. The Letter to the Hebrews says that Christ "has been tested in every respect as we are" (Heb 4:15). So deeply did he enter into our pain and degradation, that nothing human is alien to him—be it fear, or judgment, or the darkness of death. And the point in the biblical story is that precisely *this* is how he shows us the true face of the divinity.

Almost every New Testament text about his temptations makes this point. The satanic temptations at the beginning of Jesus' ministry enticed him to take the path of power and honor—use your power, turn stones into bread, throw yourself down from the pinnacle of the temple! Is it not appropriate for the Almighty to show that he has power and honor in all eternity?

Later on, Peter rejected the terrible words about suffering and death, as if these meant that Jesus himself was blaspheming against God. "This must never happen to you!" he said—speaking as it were on behalf of God. But the Master dismissed Peter's satanic temptation. In this matter, Peter lacked all sensitivity to the thoughts of God.

Then we have the final temptation: "If you are the Son of God, come down from the cross…and we will believe!" Use your power, make the heavenly hosts intervene! They mocked him: "He saved others; he cannot save himself" (Matt 27:42–43).

In the man who died on the cross, they saw only a weak God; and in one sense they were right. As the Japanese theologian Kosuke Koyama has noted,[5] the words originally meant as mockery acquire a deeper resonance in the Gospel, where they become a hidden profession of faith: "He saved others; he cannot save himself!" For that is how God is—unlike all other powers and gods. The lords and rulers of this world all know how to rescue themselves, to save their skins, to fight for their honor and victory; but they cannot save others. God is different: he saves others, but he himself is willing to perish. Christ was tortured and afflicted and mocked to death, but he prayed for his enemies and blessed those who mocked him. God lets himself be mocked.

As the Second World War was drawing to its terrible conclusion, another Japanese theologian, Kazoh Kitamori, saw how the bombs hurled with systematic precision were reducing to ruins the land he loved. People were dying of painful wounds and sicknesses, and this brought him to the insight that this wounded and sick world can be redeemed only by a Savior who himself is marked by wounds and sickness. A profound inspiration led him to write his book *The Theology of the Pain of God*. We are accustomed to saying that God's innermost dimension is love. Kitamori goes further and affirms that the innermost dimension of love is pain and weakness, the inherent contradiction generated when the One who is holy embraces those who deserve to be repulsed:

> What makes the Gospel so difficult to believe is that God acted in a way that appears to set limits to his own divinity. He acted in a manner inappropriate to God. In reality, the forgiveness of sins is just such a phenomenon. God does not repulse those who ought to be repulsed, but embraces them. It is as if God should turn out to be spineless!...This pain was the shame of the cross that God took upon himself in the person of his only-begotten Son.[6]

This vision of God refuses any theology that overlooks the pain in God. Kitamori rejects Karl Barth and his school, who make God the Absolute, so far exalted above the evil reality of the world that he remains without wounds or even scratches; such a theology takes on a hard quality, emphasizing incompatibility, exclusiveness, and rejection. Kitamori says that a God who does not embrace is a God without pain. He is of course aware of the opposite danger—that is, a cheap faith in a humane God who does not make demands and who loves without pain—and this is why he speaks of God's sacrifice. God renounced his power and honor to make space for the human person.

I do not intend to set out in detail what this entails with regard to the dialogue between Christianity and Islam. It is sometimes claimed that Islam knows nothing of God's grace and mercy, but this is incorrect; it is also true that we have much to learn from Muslims' total subjection to his will. But at the very heart of all that makes us brothers and sisters in our faith in the one God, there lies something central that divides us: the exalted and holy One, the one Creator of heaven and earth, is at the same time the One who in Christ united himself to our human existence. As the French theologian Jean Sulivan has written, "The unique grandeur of Christianity is its belief in a poor God, like a wound in the absolute....No man could invent that; it requires a revelation."[7]

We have returned to our starting point. The sandals stand at the door to the sanctuary. We must continue to visit each other's holy rooms, to listen, and to speak. Each time we leave the sanctuary, we will know a little more about each other, and perhaps a little more about God, too. We must leave it to him and to our own hearts to let the words take hold of us—provided that these words are based upon the truth. Then we will be able to meet with greater joy and trust on the streets outside the sanctuaries in the years to come.

The Shepherd and the Gurus: Christian Faith and New Age

The dust jacket of Swedish author Sven Delblanc's 1977 novel *Grottmannen* (*The Cave Dweller*) shows part of an altar reredos with Joseph and Mary kneeling in the stable. Their gaze is directed with deep devotion to the center of the picture, but the baby is not in the manger. They bow to the dust before an empty space. Adoration and longing are alive, but he is not there.

The book's main character is a modern man who has cut himself free from conventional moral norms and religious prejudices. He is divorced and has relationships with a number of women. He appears to thrive on his freedom, but emptiness gnaws at him. For all his modernity, he is drawn back to his primeval instincts, namely, the need for faith and devotion. He becomes a "cave dweller" in the modern age and is almost destroyed by the harsh discontinuity between modern ideas and old feelings:

> I am a cave dweller, I believe in something called nature. I want to lay claim to a natural order in which I do not believe, to a Hebrew God who does not exist. I want to weep over my lost son as Jacob wept over Joseph. My worldview is shining and new like a 1976 Volvo, but my feeling is as old as the prophets.' I want to own my wife. I want to own my son. I do not want to die like a solitary tree with dried-up roots.[8]

Do we not see something like this today? God has vanished out of many people's existence. The center that held things together has dissolved. People became freer, and the world seemed larger—but at the same time, it shrank. The world they attempted to master had no longer any place for the mystery. The invisible center was no longer there.

In this new world, part of our language disappeared too. People got embarrassed and their eyes began to wander as soon as religious questions arose. More than forty years ago, the Norwegian author Axel Jensen described "a confused generation afraid of the daylight, which cannot pronounce the word *God* without embarrassment—and without swearing immediately afterwards." Even blasphemy had lost its meaning, for there was no sanctuary to spit upon and no God to deny. All they were left with was a lonely feeling of loss. God belonged to a world to which they could not return, although they desperately longed for something irreplaceable that they had lost.[9]

A problem for many modern people is that they have longings and religious experience, but no vocabulary to interpret these.

Ever since my high-school days, I have found an echo of my own sentiments in the Swedish poet Pär Lagerkvist, one of the many who wanted to get rid of God but keenly felt the absence all his life. On the path that leads him away from God, he is always searching for "the spring." "I do not bend my knee before God....But I would be happy to lie down beside the spring and drink from it, to slake my thirst, my burning thirst for something I cannot grasp—yet something I know exists," he wrote in *Ahasverus död* (*Ahasuerus' Death*).[10] This is how he expresses it in a poem in his collection *Aftonland* (*Sunset Land*):[11]

> A stranger is my friend, one I do not know,
> a stranger far far away.
> Because of him, my heart is filled with distress.
> Because he is not with me.
> Because perhaps he does not exist at all?
> Who are you, that you fill my heart with your absence?
> Who fill the whole world with your absence?

Many have longings and experiences but do not know where their devotion should be directed. Their everyday thoughts have no place for God, but their deepest instincts will not allow them to rest.

Many people live in this dichotomy. If only they had a language to interpret their longing and to fill the empty space left by God...

The empty space left by God! For several decades now, we have been concerned about secularization. We have talked about "the church in a post-Christian world" and have tried to meet the modern human person who has "come of age." We have attempted to talk about Christianity in secular language. Some have spoken of a "religionless Christianity" and have conceded that "God" is dead.

We must continue to take this seriously, for we do not fully realize the consequences of the loss of God.

But this is not the whole picture. The world was not only bidding farewell to religion: simultaneously, the world was religious, indeed often desperately religious. People did not reject the church because it was too religious, but because it was not religious enough! They were searching for a presence they sensed but did not know. The church did indeed remind them of this, but they were disappointed by the superficial language used by the church, which gave answers to questions they had never asked. They met no one there who knew their souls and listened to their distress. So their longing to come home drove them away from home!

What does it signify for the church that so many have looked elsewhere for answers to their longings? Indeed, it would never occur to some people that the church might have anything to say in this domain. What is the significance of the fact that tens of thousands of young people have taken the road to India and Nepal, Tibet and Japan to search for something they did not find here at home? How do we react when we see that many who long for a "new age" deliberately conduct their search outside the Bible and Christianity, looking for alternatives in the European tradition or in other cultures? Are warnings and threats our only response?

Many people experience a spiritual poverty and petrification in the church. If we cannot appreciate this—or understand the challenges posed by the alternatives to the church—then we ought to save our breath, because all this searching not only says something about the East and the alternatives in our own culture, about the rootlessness of people today and about their longing for something better: it also says something about us. It is a prophetic word speaking of our failure. It reveals that we had no vocabulary to clothe their longings in words.

Is New Age an enrichment or a danger?

No one can seriously expect a simple answer to this question, for the New Age is so complex and inherently contradictory that it is impossible to offer an unambiguous evaluation.

In all the clutter of alternative forms of religion and views of life, there is certainly much that could enrich us. Do we not witness a genuine yearning for wholeness and coherence? Do we not see people abandoning the paralysis of materialism, dreaming of a deeper life and a more whole personality, a world of tolerance and peace? Occasionally, we perceive the longing for a divine dimension.

At the same time, much seems ephemeral and superficial. Some people have rose-colored dreams of a world at the turning point, developing almost by natural necessity in the direction of harmony and wholeness. Some expand their expectations to include cosmic experiences of interior peace and divinity. They are preoccupied with their own inner universe, but instead of being liberated, they are entangled in the labyrinths of the soul, and the world outside becomes a matter of indifference. And their perception of the divine often seems anemic, distant, something that entails no obligations. Some experiment with occult forces and, in extreme cases, have experiences that can be life threatening.

Besides this, we have all the merchants who undermine what is genuine by making money out of people's religious needs. The consumer culture so often proves to be one of the greatest dangers in the new religiosity, as we see not only in the commercialization, but also in people's restless wanderings from one movement to another in their attempts to keep up with the newest fashion and try out the newest offer on the spiritual marketplace.

And yet, despite all these critical comments, we must note that the alternative trends in religion and lifestyles have intensified many people's need to rediscover the wholeness that has disintegrated. These trends have helped define their longings and kindle their expectations—something the church has not always succeeded in doing.

⇀ ↽

Good Shepherd Sunday (the fourth Sunday of Easter) is a day in the church's calendar that invites us to special reflection, because its starting point is the image of Jesus as shepherd. One of the texts read in worship relates the dialogue in which Peter is called to be the leader of the earliest church (John 21:15–19), and this narrative can help us realize what kind of leaders we truly need. What do we expect of a "shepherd"? What is a true "master"?

One dominant characteristic of the new religiosity is the large number of masters. For many it began with the little Indian guru who smiled at us from the posters and promised world peace and inner harmony. Most people gave the Maharishi the cold shoulder, but many thousands gradually found the path to his lotus feet. After him, there have been many gurus with yoga and mantras; swamis bringing the truth about how the soul is united to the divine; Zen masters who tore away the masks so people could find their true faces; prophets with a clarity of vision who talked about auras and fields of consciousness; workshop leaders and healers with a thousand techniques for attaining self-understanding, body consciousness, and a better quality of life. They knock on the doors, put up posters on billboards, and advertise in the press and in the spirituality guidebooks. These masters are present in bookshops and in the world of industry.

I cannot go into detail about the numerous masters who have won disciples here, but the pattern reminds me of what I have seen in the East. There, I met a few who impressed me. They had been touched by something, and they possessed important insights. They helped people to lead lives that were freer and more whole. They opened up dimensions that many had forgotten.

Some genuinely made an impact on me, but there were others who made me wonder why people who were searching for truth and freedom could so quickly submit to new authorities. Were these people enticed by the huge promises? Was it because freedom had become intolerable, and they longed for someone who could eliminate the necessity of making difficult choices? Was it the solitary dream of a fellowship that gave them the feeling of wholeness?

There is no point in classifying the masters, awarding them points or ranking them. Instead, let me state why I myself always come back to *the* Master—to Christ. For I see that when other masters make an impact on me, it is because they have something that reminds me of him. And perhaps they have also offered me glimpses in which I saw him more clearly.

First, the Master is so close at hand. In the midst of everyday life, in the midst of the dirt and the smell and the struggle for existence, he is there—not as a divine "foreign body," but as a human being irradiated by love. Love flowed through his hands and glowed in his eyes. His words fell like seeds into fruitful ground. There were no extravagant gestures, no external success and riches that might have counted as signs of the divine approval as Jesus wandered the dusty roads from village to village, accompanied by friends who had had no formal education. But those with eyes to see became aware of a presence: God was in the world. They called this presence "the kingdom of God."

We sense this in Jesus's conversation with Peter. He had denied the Master three times, but Jesus did not utter one single word of rebuke. It would have been a golden opportunity to use feelings of guilt to bind Peter hand and foot, but instead, Jesus reestablishes their relationship by asking him three times: "Simon, son of John, do you love me?" Peter is given three chances to declare his love, and Jesus replies three times: "Feed my sheep." Jesus was present in the midst of the broken relationship, and he restored the wholeness.

Secondly, the Master helped people find themselves. He led them back to their starting point. He touched what was hurt, opened eyes to see new possibilities, and called them back to what they were meant to be—not by directing them to some far-off spiritual sphere, but by binding them fast to the here and now. He placed them in the world God had created. The Swedish hymn writer Anders Frostenson has written:

> God's love is like shore and grass,
> with wind and breadth and all the wide universe...
> We want a freedom where we are ourselves,
> a freedom we can do something with,
> where there is no emptiness, but space for dreams,
> an earth where trees and flowers can take root.[12]

Jesus offered no rose-colored dreams of cosmic breakthroughs and divinity. For why should we devote our energies to living in some spiritual sphere when the real problem is to take root and blossom where we actually are? Why seek something superhuman when the challenge is to become truly human?

Thirdly, the Master led people away from themselves. Unlike all the dreams of inner peace and harmony, his teaching showed that a meaningful life is not to be measured in terms of well-being and success. The important point is to be good, to live aright. He knew that the kingdom of heaven was not to be found in inner bliss, but in fellowship. Frostenson writes in his hymn:

> As yet, there are walls between us,
> and we stretch out hands through a wire fence.
> Stones of fear form the walls of our prison room,
> our prison clothing is our shuttered self.

Jesus taught his disciples that such a fellowship could mean pain and sacrifices—he himself was the shepherd who laid down his life for the flock. He said that only the one who let go of himself would find himself. Church history teaches us that the greatest were those who became what they were meant to be by renouncing themselves. In his conversation with Peter, Jesus showed that the disciple's future as shepherd would mean an end to an easy life: until now, Peter had made his own decisions, but one day others would lead him where he did not want to go. Tradition relates that Peter, like his Master, died on a cross.

There is something disturbing about the Master. The freedom of which he speaks, the freedom he brings into the world, binds us to others. There is a lot here that goes against the grain of our instincts and dreams. We long for a wholeness that will give harmony, and our dreams transport us away from pain and tensions. In general, we try to avoid difficulties. But he issues a challenge to our instincts and appeals to something yet more whole, yet more true, with its origins in the very depths of our humanity. For it is the *whole* of reality that is embraced by our relationship to God: both the inner world with its longings and good dreams, mixed with everything that is ugly, crippled, and destroyed; and the outer world with God's creative presence and devilry and destruction. This is where we must live.

God's creative dreams for the world entail a wholeness that is not achieved by amputating all that is ugly and unwished for, nor by closing our eyes to it or suppressing it. When the Master describes God's perfection, he does not mention his purity and exalted holiness, but speaks of a wholeness that can accommodate the opposite of love, by loving one's enemies and blessing one's opponents. He enters the chaotic diversity of the world and says that *this* is God's world, and he wants to create something with this world.

It is this Master who makes it possible—and important—to hold fast to the church. It may indeed be true that the church has overshadowed him, suppressed his demands, and drowned him out with its nebulous words and rites. Nevertheless, the church is the place where his words have been audible for two thousand years. Because this word is heard, told again and again and celebrated, the church is also the place where God can create something new: a new language, a new presence, with wholeness and solidarity, and perhaps a new unease.

In one of his essays, the Norwegian author Jens Bjørneboe expresses a longing I believe many bear deep down in their hearts: "We may mock Christianity, scorn it, and find it revolting—but the day we draw aside the veil that covers it, we will recognize the beloved of our young days, and our only true love."[13]

Where are we in all this?

Some may stand before the altar reredos and join Joseph and Mary in looking with astonishment at the manger where the child is missing. Some do not miss this child in the slightest. But many have a feeling of loss. They are paralyzed by his absence, torn between departure from God and yearning for God. Some have traveled far in order to fill the empty space with a new meaning.

Ultimately, all I can do is point to the Master, for he *is* there. He is present, alive, and challenging. If we open our eyes and look, he may begin to live among us.

The challenge this entails was once formulated by a Japanese Zen Buddhist who visited a Christian monastery in Europe and followed the monastic rhythm for several weeks. Finally, the monks had lived through the paschal mystery in the texts and rites of the liturgy. Early on Easter morning—before the sun dawned on the day of resurrection—the monastery was abruptly woken to life by this Zen monk who ran along the corridors, beating a drum like a man gone mad and crying out again and again: "I want to see Christ risen in you! I want to see Christ risen in you!"

The Wind Blows Where It Wills

Many associate Pentecost with excited feelings. The words flow freely, bodies tremble, the mood reaches a breaking point: When will the hour of the Lord come, with fire from on high? Where is the storm wind of the Spirit?

John tells us of another kind of Pentecost. Here there is no storm wind, just the quiet whisper of astonishment; no ecstatic shakings or music with irresistible rhythms, just "deep tones at dawn and at eve" that "touch even the heart as hard as rock," as the Danish poet N.F.S. Grundtvig puts it in his Pentecost hymn. We could perhaps call this an "inner ecstasy."

Two people meet late at night. Under cover of darkness, a learned rabbi has found the way to Jesus's lodgings. Jesus was visiting Jerusalem, and John tells us that he "would not entrust himself" to the other pilgrims, "for he himself knew what was in everyone." However, Jesus must have seen hidden depths in the counselor Nicodemus, for he cuts through the small talk and goes straight to the fundamental questions: How can I see the kingdom of God? How can I be born anew? "Very truly, I tell you, no one can enter the kingdom of God without being born of water and Spirit," says Jesus. He underlines this point: "What is born of the flesh is flesh, and what is born of the Spirit is spirit. Do not be astonished that I said to you, 'You must be born anew.' The wind blows where it chooses, and you hear the sound of it, but you do not know where it comes from or where it goes. So it is with everyone who is born of the Spirit" (John 3:1–10).

The conversation creates a silent space around the two men. The darkness vanishes and the simple room becomes a sanctuary where there opens up an endless series of vaults behind vaults. Indirectly, the narrative reveals that Nicodemus's great learning had not helped him: he asks, "How can these things be?" And Jesus replies, "Are you a teacher of Israel, and yet you do not understand these things?"

This recalls something a Christian mystic once wrote about his own search. He had looked for God with a lamp that shone so brightly that everyone else envied him. He sought God in the stars and in the tiniest mousehole. He sought him in libraries and universities. He sought God with a telescope and a microscope…until one day he realized that he had forgotten what he was looking for. "Then I extinguished my lamp and threw away my keys and began to weep," he said. "In that moment he was there, shining in my heart."[14]

Nicodemus sought the light under cover of darkness. He had studied scripture all his life, and knew every nook and cranny of the Bible. He had learned to ask the right questions, and he was familiar with the answers. He knew what fidelity was—the persevering longing for the living God. The ancient words had followed him throughout his life, just as they have followed the Jews throughout their history as their principal profession of faith: "Hear, O Israel: The LORD is our God, the LORD alone. You shall love the LORD your God with all your heart, and with all your soul, and with all your might" (Deut 6:5). These words are often referred to as the *shema* ("Hear!"). They were whispered into Nicodemus's ear at his birth, and they had accompanied him in his daily prayers. He heard them in times of sorrow and in times of gladness. They would be on his lips as he drew his last breath. *Shema*—"Hear!"—reminded the Jews unceasingly that God was the shining center of their existence. Nicodemus bore these words in leather phylacteries on his arm and his forehead. They were written on the doorposts of his house and on his gates. They have accompanied the Jews up to the present day. They have been whispered and cried out, in sighing or in exultation. They were spoken when millions of Jews were gassed in Hitler's death camps.

"You shall love the Lord your God with all your heart, and with all your soul, and with all your might!" Nicodemus knew this. Indeed, he could explain these words to others. And yet, he was still waiting for them to shine in his own heart.

In the Bible, darkness symbolizes that which is formless, chaotic, and threatening. The creation narrative says that "the earth was a formless void, and darkness covered the deep." But God's Spirit moved over the waters, and the light was created. Thus creation began: chaos became cosmos, the world took on color and form, and God penetrated everything with his breath, so that it became alive.

Was a process of creation beginning in Nicodemus's dark world? Had the chaos hidden under his well-ordered surface become intolerable to him? He felt afraid of the inner unrest that was cracking up and threatening to break out. But it was the opposite that happened: through the cracks, the light began to filter *in*. The Spirit blew over the mighty deep.

There is an obvious ambiguity here. The Bible is playing with words: *Spirit* and *wind*, the breath of life and human breathing. The Greek word *pneuma* means both "spirit" and "wind." Our translation of John says, "The wind blows where it chooses." We could equally well read, "The Spirit blows where he chooses. You hear the sound of him, but you do not know where he comes from or where he is going. So it is with everyone who is born of the wind."

"As long as my breath is in me and the spirit of God is in my nostrils," says Job (27:3). The Psalmist (104:29–30) says:

> When you take away their breath, they die
> and return to their dust.
> When you send forth your spirit, they are created;
> and you renew the face of the ground.

Isaiah (42:5) sees the Creator shaping the firmament of heaven and spreading out the earth with everything that grows upon it:

> [He] who gives breath to the people upon it
> and spirit to those who walk in it.

Perhaps these three had observed the moist winds coming like a breath of new life over the dry fields, with clouds and rain that watered the earth and made things grow. The Spirit is the breath of life and of the new creation.

In the creation narratives, we read how God blew the breath of life into the nostrils of the human, who thus became a living soul (Gen 2:7). An old legend relates that Jesus as a child modeled birds of clay and breathed on them so that they came alive and flew away. These images may be simple, almost primitive expressions for the vital force, but they speak to the depths in us. In his account of Jesus' resurrection, John writes in similar terms that Jesus breathed on the disciples and said: "Receive the Holy Spirit." His breath was a new creation.

This language crosses all boundaries and finds a profound echo in the East. The Indians speak of *atman*, the human soul that seeks the divine; this word may be familiar to us from the German verb *atmen*, "to breathe." The vital breath of the human person, his *atman* or spirit, seeks the divine. The same idea is found in Chinese tradition, in which the breath or vital energy of the human person seeks the rhythm in the breathing of the universe. It is not by chance that breathing plays such an important role in

Eastern meditation. When a Christian friend of mine sought instruction in meditation from a Japanese Buddhist master, he was told: "From now, you must breathe Christ. Breathe in the Holy Spirit. Then come and tell me what meditation is!"

Something similar is found in Polynesia, too. For thousands of years, the wind has formed both physical and spiritual life for those who live on the Pacific islands. The wind brings rain, cereal crops, and life. The wind fills the sails and makes fishing, travel, and communication possible. Wind and breath and spirit are the fundamental principle of life.

Let us reflect on the winds that blew into Nicodemus's life. Perhaps we shall also feel their breath in our own minds.

Some are disturbed by Jesus's words: "What is born of the flesh is flesh, and what is born of the Spirit is spirit." Is he speaking of two types of human being—those equipped with religious talents and those whose nature is that of spiritual illiterates? That is hardly what Jesus wants to say. Rather, these words seem to be asking a question about how we encounter life, an urgent appeal to open ourselves to the breath of life—let the Spirit blow, let the earth be moistened so the grain can grow! Be aware of the wind that whispers over the depths in your mind!

Nicodemus was well instructed in his religion. "You shall love the LORD your God with all your heart, and with all your soul, and with all your might." Like a field full of corn, he was full of knowledge of the Bible and explanations of its texts, but he was still waiting for it to sprout. How can I see the kingdom of God? How can I be born anew? Jesus replies: Let the Spirit blow. Let the wind come from on high with its life-giving rain, so that all you know and all the potential you bear within you can sprout and grow and bear fruit.

It may be that the Spirit's breath had reached Nicodemus even before he sought advice from Jesus, for the words that had been whispered into his ear when he was a child were living words, formed in tenderness, which had coalesced with the rhythm of human breathing to become sounds, a prayer and a blessing, whenever the breath vibrated through the throats of those who uttered them. The vibration was still in the words. But words that are spirit when they are spoken can turn into dead letters, lifeless like seeds in dry ground.

So the learned counselor sought the counsel of an unlearned carpenter who said that he came from God. Did Nicodemus recognize in Jesus's words something of the breath of life those words had had when they were first sown in his mind? He needed someone to open up the springs and water the earth so that what he knew through his scholarship might be reborn and grow anew.

This is perhaps not so very far from our own experience. Our learning and our knowledge of the Bible do indeed vary. Some have a field full of corn—quotations from scripture, fragments of narrative, verses and motifs from the psalms, perhaps half-forgotten experiences. Most of us have something, at any rate.

This, however, can seem dead: words from a book, lines and signs on paper, sounds that cross our lips automatically. We all have periods in our life when the wind begins to whisper—perhaps as a vague unease, a distant memory that flashes through our mind, a hidden fear that life is slipping through our hands before we have even learned how to live it, a longing for something different. We can drown this out by means of words and evasions, friendly advice and warnings, activity and noise. But when the noise dies down and the friendly advice falls silent, the wind continues to whisper. It blows life into biblical verses we thought we had forgotten. It turns up in dreams and surprises us in unguarded moments. Finally, the vague perceptions coalesce with our own breathing and pass through our throats as questions and prayers from our very depths: How is life to become meaningful? Is it time to be born?

A Jewish legend relates what happened when God revealed his name to Moses. He had already revealed himself as *Yahweh*, which means "I am" or "I am the one I am" (Exod 3:14); but the legend relates that God disclosed yet another name, a name so simple that everyone would remember it, even unlearned persons who had no insight, or else did not understand Hebrew. Moses was told that God's name was *Yaaaah*. This is the name of the deep breathing, and that is enough. That name would resound in the Jews' huts in their Egyptian slavery, it would coalesce with the sighs from all in the world who despaired and yearned, it would be heard when sufferers expressed their pain in groans. And then God himself, Yaaaah, would be close at hand, with hope and new life.

Nicodemus is mentioned on two later occasions. Once, he attempts to get his colleagues to give Jesus a fair trial. The second time, he is present when Jesus's body is taken down from the cross. He has with him one hundred pounds of scented ointment, a mixture of myrrh and aloes. That amounts to more than thirty-two kilograms of precious ointment! Was this an expression of thanks to the Master who had taught him to live? Was it the generous gift of a learned man to the unlearned man who had opened his mind?

We do not know. But we perceive the rebirth of a man who had experienced a different kind of Pentecost: the still whispering of amazement, the inner ecstasy that is born in the song of praise after the unrest of the night.

To an Unknown God...

An old legend tells what happened after Adam and Eve, on the day they were created, had rebelled against God and were driven out of the Garden of Eden. When they saw the sun set for the first time, they were terrified, since they interpreted the darkness as a sign that the world was being destroyed because of their guilt. They both wept and sat facing each other throughout that terrible night. When morning dawned, their hearts were transformed. Adam stood up, captured an animal, and offered it as a sacrifice instead of himself.

In all cultures and periods, people have built altars for their gods. We find the simplest signs of the divine presence and power: rough-hewn stones, symbols of sex and fertility, a mound in the earth, a tree, a picture—or else beautiful altars of stone and wood, decorated with flowers and tendrils and exuberant symbols. We find altars out in the open, exposed to wind and weather and worn down by the elements. Others are erected inside sanctuaries: a dwelling for the god, a temple with walls and columns, a cathedral with arches reaching up toward heaven and hidden vaults.

Paul had spent some days in Athens, getting to know the city and observing the life that teemed there. He had strolled through the sanctuaries, speaking with the people he met and making contact with wise men and philosophers. The Acts of the Apostles says that the Athenians were curious people: both they "and the foreigners living there would spend their time in nothing but telling or hearing something new." The philosophers challenge Paul to give an account of his new teaching and meet him on the Areopagus, a well-known location for political and religious discussions. It is a trial of strength, with one faith matched against another, and Paul's Areopagus speech repays our attention (Acts 17:22–34).

He begins thus: "Athenians, I see how extremely religious you are in every way." His words indicate a willingness to understand them, but at the same time, there is a critical undertone—for the Greek word has another nuance, and we could also translate: "I see how extremely superstitious you are." It is obvious that Paul had his problems with the Athenians' religion. He was appalled by all their gods. A man from a Jewish background could never accept all their attempts to create images of the invisible. The One who is holy cannot be portrayed in images, and it is scarcely possible to pronounce his name without desecrating it.

Only at one point does Paul adopt a milder tone. In the midst of all their superstition, he had noticed an altar with the inscription: "To an unknown god." Here he finds something positive that he can latch onto: perhaps their religiosity has the potential for deeper insights.

This dual possibility says something important. Religiosity is ambiguous; indeed, it is often open to a whole number of interpretations. Religiosity blinds people and gives them the power of sight; it creates and it destroys. Religion hardens people's hearts, but it can also make them gentle and receptive. One can be very religious—and one can also be very superstitious.

We do not know exactly what this altar was. It may have been an expression of superstitious fear: in order to be completely sure that no divinity or power should feel excluded, the Athenians built an extra altar for the unknown powers, a guarantee for safety's sake. Perhaps it was a sanctuary for foreigners: if they were given an altar for their gods, this would stimulate trade and promote mutual understanding. Or was the altar the expression of a longing for something deeper and truer that lay beyond the myriad divinities in the Greek pantheon?

Paul chooses to take the last interpretation as his starting point. It may be right to say that he employs a cheap rhetorical trick in order to get the conversation going; he knows what he wants to say, and he quickly reaches the point: "What therefore you worship as unknown, this I proclaim to you." And he begins to speak about the risen Christ.

In the course of his address, however, Paul says something about God that goes deeper than any rhetorical devices or figures of speech: God does not dwell in temples. God's presence does not depend on buildings, divine images, rites, or specific religious practices. He does not need any of the things with which we worship him, for the whole world is his, and it is he who gives life and breath and all things. God has scattered human beings across the face of the earth in order that they might search for him, though indeed he is not far from each one of us. He is here, Paul says, as you yourselves know. Your own poets have spoken about this: one of them wrote, "For we too are his offspring." Another poet wrote: "It is in him we live and move and have our being." So do not shut the living God away in temples, do not exchange him for images of gold and silver and stone! He cannot be localized. The whole world is not able to contain him, yet he is here for those who have eyes to see.

This means that Paul has taken significant steps toward his listeners and follows them into their own world. This is not only a question of quoting from their own poets: the Athenians recognize themselves when he refers to the Bible too. He paints a picture of the Creator who gives life to all things, who forms us in his own image and blows the breath of life into us, so that we can live and develop our potential. We are dependent on God's breath: it is in his breathing that we too live and breathe (cf. Ps 104:29–30).

Did the Athenians begin to wonder at this point whether Paul was one of them? They could almost have said what he said, word for word. Some modern readers might object that Paul's words sound pantheistic—his words suggest the idea that God is present in everything; but Paul is appealing here not least to the Stoic appreciation of the divine reason that penetrates the whole of reality. The Stoics maintained that, although many divinities were worshiped, behind them all lay the One; and all things are shaped by the laws of nature. It is in the innermost nature of things that we live and move and have our being.

Let us leave the Areopagus for a while. Paul is halfway through his speech. He has his audience thinking. He has met them in their own world, and none of them knows as yet where all this is leading. We will let them ponder his words for a while, before we come back to Athens and resume our reflections.

In the meantime, we take Paul further east. He joins the teeming throng in India's holy places—or still further east, in the towns and sanctuaries in China and Japan. He has wandered through their temples and found much to surprise him. He has asked questions of people in the marketplaces and has talked with ascetics and wise men.

What would Paul have said, if they had challenged him? Would he have followed them into their world in the same way as in Athens? He would certainly have been shocked by their idols—innumerable portraits of gods and powers, both beautiful and grotesque, gentle and terrifying, animal and human, divinities in all the colors of the rainbow, gods who protect and gods who destroy. He would have cast his eyes to the ground when he saw explicit portrayals of sex and potency side by side with an ascetic flight from the world. He would have been confused by the contrast between the silence of their meditation and the noisy rites of popular religion.

But perhaps he would have begun in the same way: "Indians! Friends from the East! I see how extremely religious you are in every way." Some would notice his undertone: "I see how extremely superstitious you are in every way." Paul would continue: "As I wandered around in your temples, I found a longing for something truer, something lying beneath all the multiplicity on the surface. Not an altar with an inscription honoring an unknown god, as in Athens, but an intense yearning to be led from that which is mortal to that which is immortal, from the unreal to the real, as your own wise men so finely put it."

Perhaps he would take up the incipient perceptions in their ancient writings that, behind the various divinities, there is one power holding them all together: "That which is true is One, although the wise use many different names," says the Rig Veda (1:169). Or perhaps he would even dare to take up the principal tradition in Eastern thinking, which sees the divine as the vital force in all things. Brahman—the divine—is the vital principle behind the external surface, the same as the *atman* that the human person recognizes in his innermost being. Make a cut in a tree at its roots and the sap will flow. Cut it higher up on the trunk or in its topmost branches, and the sap will still flow, because it is alive. But when life abandons the tree, it will wither. That which has lost the vital force dies, but life itself does not die. The divine is the innermost subtle substance that penetrates everything, and that is what Brahman is.

Paul might perhaps say: "I see that you have a unique sensitivity to the divine presence. It is in the divinity that we live and move and have our being. God scattered us over the face of the earth in order that we might seek him, and perhaps find the path back to our own origin. As you yourselves say: 'The deepest dimension in the human being seeks the divine.'"

Here too, they would perhaps be surprised that one from the far-off West, a Jew who believed in Christ, had such a profound insight that they could recognize their own deepest longings in what he said.

Let us return to the Areopagus. Paul is beginning to formulate his first conclusion: "Since we are God's offspring, we ought not to think that the deity is like gold, or silver, or stone, an image formed by the art and imagination of mortals."

They are still keeping up with his train of thought. The people may indeed have their divinities and their superstition, but the wise men have seen something deeper: the divine is a reality that goes beyond all that we can create in our human art and imagination.

But now comes the parting of the ways. Both Greeks and people from eastern Asia would expect Paul to follow them further at this point, and to affirm that the divine is the eternal and immutable vital principle lying behind all things, the invisible power that flows through everything; and they would add that correspondingly, the deepest dimension in the human person shares in the divine nature. After all, Paul himself had said that "we are his offspring"! And this means that redemption consists of getting in touch with the divine, which lies in the deepest region of the soul's secret chamber. Search within yourself, therefore, liberate yourself from the captivity of the body, and rise up to the divine origin! As the drop is absorbed into the ocean and becomes one with it, the soul must be set free from all that is external, so that it can become one with the eternal.

Many of his listeners are shocked when Paul presents *his* version: They have not completely known the God for whom they searched and longed, the God who is as close to them as their life and breath. He is no eternal law regulating life, no impersonal power flowing through the universe. On the contrary, says Paul, he is a personal God. He speaks to us, seeks us, and calls us by name. He loves us as a father loves his children, and he watches over us as a mother watches over the child at her breast. Indeed, we can go further than this: the invisible God has shown us his face, though not in idols and things produced by human art and imagination. It is in Jesus Christ, a human being of flesh and blood, that God has revealed in luminous clarity who he is. He entered human beings' lives, dried their tears, held them by the hand, fought against injustice, ate and drank with the hopeless and the outcasts, and exposed his own heart. What therefore you worship as unknown, this I proclaim to you, Paul continues: God has made himself known in Jesus Christ. He was born in a manger, shared his life with ordinary human beings, died on a cross, and rose from

the dead. *He* is God's face in the world. It is he whom we shall
meet as our judge at the resurrection of the dead.

We notice that the assembly has fallen silent. Initially, they
are indeed speechless—does Paul actually mean what he is saying? Then they understand, and they begin to protest in a storm
of indignation and mockery. He is going too far! Was this all the
"babbler" had to offer—new gods and foreign superstition? As if
we did not have enough of that in this city already!

However, the text continues: "Others said, 'We will hear you
again about this.'" And some "joined him and became believers"
(Acts 17:32–34).

What had the Athenians understood? What was Paul trying to say
when he linked faith in God to Jesus? What do we mean when we
speak of a personal God? This was certainly something that divided
the biblical religion from the ideas about the divine that Paul
encountered on the Areopagus and that are found in so many variations in the East and in modern religiosity.

Here, we are helped by other texts that supply depth and
perspective when we seek to understand the personal dimension
of faith in God. The divine mystery cannot be contained in any
of our words and ideas. Nevertheless, we dare to speak of God as
a personal God.

When God called Moses to lead the people out of Egypt,
his initial reaction was to refuse this vocation. He knew, of course,
that the One who spoke was the God of Abraham, Isaac, and
Jacob, the God whom his ancestors had worshiped. But Moses
protested that the people would not listen to him—what is the
point of saying that the God of their ancestors has sent me, when
I do not even know his name? Here is my name, answers the
Lord: "I AM WHO I AM." In the Old Testament, the interpretation is derived from the divine name itself. *Yahweh* means "I am."
"Thus you shall say to the Israelites, I AM has sent me to you."

If God's name is "I am who I am," ought not that to mean that God is the One who exists eternally behind all that is changeable, the force that permeates all things and is the innermost essence in the human person himself—as the Greeks and Indians would say? Certainly! These words identify God as the source and origin of life. We can turn our backs on him, but we can never detach ourselves completely from him, since it is in him we live and move and have our being. We exist in the divine "I am."

But these very words, like the biblical narratives as a whole, point in another direction: Yahweh is no impersonal force. He is not a passive and immutable existence, but a reality that is active and life-giving. The name *I am* means that it is he who makes things exist, the One who creates and bestows life. The God of whom the Bible speaks intervenes in history, fights against injustice, liberates the oppressed, and leads into freedom.

Last but not least: When God says, "I am," he says to the human person, "You are," "You are to go," as we see so clearly in the story of Moses. And this allows the human person to rise up and say his own "I am." Our "I am" is not the same as God's "I am." God *gives* life, and the human person *receives* life as a gift. There is an eternal bond between God and the human person, but they are not identical. To be his offspring does not mean that we are divine, but that we have our origin in him. My vocation as a human being is not to be absorbed into the divinity as the drop is absorbed into the ocean, but to become a true human being—and this I do when I stand up and meet him, answer him when he addresses me, and seek his face.

Why does Paul end his discourse by speaking of Jesus? It is because *he* gave the Eternal a face. Paul knows that God is not held captive in images and ideas created by human beings. God does not dwell in temples. The world is filled with his glory, and he does not need any of the things with which we can serve him, not even the altars we set up to atone for our guilt and to quiet our fears; for it was he himself who offered the perfect sacrifice when, in Christ, he descended and shared in our human lot and bore our guilt. The only meaningful altar is the one we build to celebrate his presence and to praise what he has done.

Some mocked Paul. But others said: "We will hear you again about this."

The Witnesses

One of the great Jewish wise men, a Chassidic rabbi in seventeenth-century Poland, went out late one night to wander through the streets of the city. He met another wanderer and called out: "My friend, why are you out so late at night? What are you doing? For whom are you working?" The other man replied, "I am a watch-man. My work consists of going around and reminding people. I remind them of events and of dangers, and I tell them about the time and the weather." "Ah yes, of course," said the wise man, and made to continue on his way. But then it was the watchman's turn to put a question: "You too are out late at night, rabbi. What are you doing? And for whom are you working?" After a moment's silence, the wise man replied: "Tell me, watchman, are you willing to become my servant?" He answered: "What would my job be, if I became your servant?" And the rabbi replied: "Your only task would be to remind me. Again and again, you would have to remind me of those two questions: What are you doing? For whom are you working?"

Two days in the year—November 1, All Saints Day, and November 2, All Souls Day—have a particularly clear function as days that remind us. We celebrate these days both in order to be reminded, and to remind others. They are days of remembrance. When we think of those who have gone on ahead of us, we are not only reminded of former times; we are confronted with the life we lead today, and with the question: What are we doing with this life?

For most of us, these days are linked with people we have loved. In many countries, such as Norway and Germany, people visit the cemeteries and light a candle on the graves of their loved ones. They look back, speak quiet words about the dead, and wish them eternal rest. This is a wonderful tradition.

And yet, on All Saints and All Souls, the center of gravity lies elsewhere. Naturally, those whom we have loved are a part of this celebration, but our perspective is much wider. On All Saints Day, we think of all the witnesses to the faith, that great fellowship of men and women whom we call "saints." For Protestants, this term is not restricted to those whom the church has canonized so that they bear the title "saint." Rather, it applies to the great throng of believers who have "finished the race," those whose lives were rooted in the reality of God's forgiveness. Their lives bore witness to this, so that they made his presence visible in dramatic events and in everyday life. Most of them are nameless, but some are remembered in a special way, because they lived their faith more strongly, more clearly, or more brightly than others.

The Letter to the Hebrews speaks rather obscurely of a "cloud of witnesses" from the righteous Abel to Christ (Heb 11:1—12:3).

There is something strange about these witnesses. They were not "successful" heroes of the faith who got what they wanted in life, and who then were able to rest on their laurels. Their lives were a constant act of defiance, in faith and in hope. The author of Hebrews presents a whole list of people from earlier times who never received any visible evidence of their faith. They never actually attained the fulfillment of their promises. Abraham believed in God's promises and left his native land, but he never settled as an inhabitant of the land God had given him. In faith, Moses refused to lead a prosperous life at Pharaoh's court and preferred to suffer along with God's people—yet he died at the border of the promised land. The great witnesses died without seeing the realization of the promises they had received; but their expectation lived on:

> [Some] were tortured, refusing to accept release, in order to attain a better resurrection. Others suffered mocking and flogging, and even chains and imprisonment. They were stoned to death, they were sawn in two, they were killed by the sword; they went about in skins of sheep and goats, destitute, persecuted, tormented—of whom the world was not worthy. They wandered in deserts and mountains, and in caves and holes in the ground. (Heb 11:35–38)

These words were addressed to Christians who risked losing heart—their faith had become a burden that cost more than they had reckoned on, and they longed desperately to have some proof of what they believed in. Did they not profess that Christ had risen from the dead and taken his seat at the right hand of the Father? Had they not heard that everything was laid under his feet? Why then did they not see any visible signs of this victory?

The author of the letter confirms their observations when he writes: "As it is, we do not yet see everything in subjection to him" (Heb 2:8). He knows that tribulation is wearing them down; he sees how some are withdrawing and defying their leaders. They forget their fellow Christians who are being persecuted. Some are tempted by doctrines that cost less and promise more—all they would have to do is turn to angels and to lower divine forces.

Now comes the reminder: the witnesses! For whom are you working? What do you want to do with your life? Look at those who have gone ahead, believing despite all the difficult circumstances. Indeed, look at Jesus who is the source of our faith and brings it to fulfilment. He bore the cross and paid no heed to the disgrace. Could there be anything "higher" than following him down into his degradation en route to the goal? Following him means keeping love alive, practicing hospitality even when it puts one's own life at risk, and remembering those in prison as if one were in prison together with them. Faith means solidarity: "Think of those who are being tortured—for you have bodies too" (Heb 13:1–3).

Here, I must recall a conversation in Japan some years ago. I met a simple, noble person who triggered my memory. He had never put his foot inside a church door, but he spoke about Christ with glowing eyes: "Christ! A man who loved so intensely could never grow old. He had to die young. But he received a wonderful resurrection in return!"

We talked about the good life. I observed that it was difficult to live one's faith in daily life, following Jesus in his unconditional love, obedience, and sacrifice. He looked at me and asked, in his intense manner: "But wasn't that precisely why we were born? Didn't you receive your life in order that you could give it away?" I must admit that I jumped in my chair and looked at him skeptically. Obviously, he had learned all the right words! But there was nothing false about him. He was not attempting to teach someone who ought to know better. What he said came from his heart—from "a true Israelite without deceit," as Jesus said about Nathanael (John 1:47). I myself felt more like Nicodemus, the learned scribe who came to Jesus by night to talk about the new birth, when Jesus asked him: "Are you a teacher of Israel, and yet you do not understand these things?" (John 3:10).

Naturally, I *knew* all these things. What happened was that a witness *reminded* me and brought me back to reality, and his words live within me still, years later—not as a burden, nor with that uneasy feeling of being a failure that we often get when someone tells us the truth, but as inspiration and as the power I need to return to the most important questions of all: For whom are you working? What are you doing with your life?

In one of the texts read on All Saints Day, Jesus sketches the picture of a church which does not exist for its own sake alone: "You are the salt of the earth; but if salt has lost its taste, how can its saltness be restored? It is no longer good for anything, but is thrown out and trampled under foot. You are the light of the world. A city built on a hill cannot be hid. No one after lighting a lamp puts it under the bushel basket, but on the lampstand, and it gives light to all in the house. In the same way, let your light shine before others, so that they may see your good works and give glory to your Father in heaven" (Matt 5:13–16).

Salt—people have known for generations that salt preserves. Without salt, meat and foodstuffs would be spoiled. In a warm climate, the flies would soon be swarming as the stench of rotten meat spread. You are salt in the world. Your call is to prevent the world from rotting, to hold back destruction.

And light—do we not often feel that the light is flickering and on the point of going out? The terrible wars in our world are a darkness that drives us to despondency and wears down our faith. Are there no limits to evil and ugliness? Are hatred and the thirst for revenge so strong that there is no place for pardon and reconciliation? The darkness is so overwhelming.

Salt and light, says Jesus. He was speaking to people who themselves were victims of circumstances. He had declared them "blessed" because they bore the burdens of life without forgetting the meaning of life. To be blessed does not mean that one sails with a favorable wind, encountering only happiness and success on one's route. It means that one is blessed by going on the paths of God despite what this costs. Jesus is talking to people who bear burdens: they mourn and suffer injustice, they are persecuted and slandered, they are poor. But they hold out, preserving mercy and purity of heart. They thirst for righteousness and make peace.

They are despised, but they are blessed. They are the salt of the earth. The wretched ones are the light of the world.

Salt and light. Can we believe that the light is stronger than the darkness, that the rot can be checked? And not least: when we hear Jesus tell the disciples that they are the light and salt of the world, can we grasp that these words apply to *us*? Dare we join the group? Dare we say that God's church is light and salt in this world?

The words are so tremendous that we hesitate. We look at the church, we look at ourselves—and we see pettiness and cheating, halfheartedness, dejection, and our own mixed-up lives. Are *we* supposed to be signs? We do not often have the feeling that we are putting a halt to the darkness and the rot!

But then something breaks through our dispiritedness and shows us our lives in a larger perspective—the reminder! What are you doing? For whom are you working? We see the cloud of witnesses who surround us, we see the radiant forms of those men and women of prayer, the thousands who persevered under persecution, sources of strength and bearers of light, mystics and thinkers, visionaries who point the way ahead, Francis of Assisi and all the others who brought light to people who knew nothing other than the stench of poverty and the plague. The external circumstances were impossible, and yet they lived the good news in our world. They are witnesses who give us courage and hope, calling us back to life: What are you really doing? For whom are you working?

Toward the end of the Second World War, the German theologian Dietrich Bonhoeffer was arrested. Two years later, he was executed because of his opposition to Hitler. His struggle translated into real life what he had written, a few years earlier, about taking up the cross and following Jesus. He asked: What is the light that is meant to shine and make the cross visible? And he answered: It is the works Jesus accomplishes in his disciples when he makes them the light of the world under his cross. "The cross becomes visible, and the works of the cross become visible. The wretchedness and the renunciation of those pronounced blessed become visible. But the cross, and a church like this, cannot lead to the praise of human beings, but only to the praise of God."[15]

Listen to Dag Hammarskjöld's testimony in *Vägmärken* (*Markings*), the journal that was published only after the General Secretary of the United Nations was shot down as he flew over the African jungle on a peace mission. This book gives us glimpses of a Christian who saw his work as a vocation: "Goodness is really very simple: to be there for other people always, and never to seek one's own self."[16]

It was said that if the Korean poet Kim Chi Ha was silenced, this would amount to ripping out the tongues of a million Koreans. He became the voice of the people in a totalitarian state whose weapons were the secret police, violence, and emergency laws:

> My blood cries out:
> Reject!
> All lies and falsehood—
> reject them![17]

Under torture, he was compelled to "confess" that he was a Catholic and a communist, but later he managed to smuggle out a letter to his friends: "I am shut in a dark solitary cell, without permission to write or to read—not even the Bible. I spend every day in meditation, surrounded by these gloomy walls. But my spirit is closer to the Lord than ever before....As long as the Lord is at my side and you continue your indomitable struggle out there, I do not complain about these tribulations that the Lord has sent me as a sign of his divine will."[18]

The Brazilian archbishop Helder Camara worked all his life for the poor in his diocese, although the death squads continually threatened reprisals. One collection of his reflections bears the title *A Thousand Reasons for Living*:

Why fear the night?
Ought we not rather to love it
when it comes to us with the stars?
And who knows
if it is not precisely on the darkest nights
that the stars clothe themselves
in their greatest splendor?[19]

We could mention many other names, but most remain nameless for us, like the grandmothers who risked their lives by defying the weapons and the violence of their mighty oppressors in order to find their children and grandchildren in the prisons and torture chambers of Latin America.

What is it about them that makes our hearts glow? Why does their courageous commitment not make us despondent? Is it not because we know, deep down, that their testimony is true? Is it not because they nourish faith and hope in us, and call us to discipleship? They teach us that the meaning of life is to exist for others.

All Saints Day. A cloud of witnesses. The great burning light, the Master himself who is the origin of our faith and brings it to fulfillment—but also all the others, from the great witnesses about whom we sing and for whom we give thanks, to the small flickering lights that just manage to survive in the darkness.

We celebrate their memory. We take them into our lives as a reminder of the only questions that matter: What are we doing with our lives? For whom are we working?

III

OUT OF THE DEPTHS...

Out of the depths I cry to you, O LORD.
Lord, hear my voice!
(Psalm 130)

silence is not
existence without noises
rooms without windows and children
life without thoughts or pains
silence is
when your voice penetrates
through all that is
as it is wont to be
and is transformed
into a gentle
caress of love in my heart
(Finn Bjørnseth, Norwegian poet)[1]

"My Soul Cries Out to You..."

I have a painting in my house that shows a path winding into the landscape until it disappears from sight in the center of the picture, in a dark wood. In the hinterground, steep mountains are turning blue, and the sky can only just be glimpsed at their summits.

As we follow the path inward toward the center, we discover that we have lost the overview. We thought we were on course, we thought we had a goal and a direction. And did we not also perceive the presence of something greater?

Now, we no longer know. We stand there, confused, in the center of the picture, and do not know where we ought to go. Have we taken a wrong turn? Ought we to continue on into the unknown, taking the chance that the path is passable, or should we try to return to our starting point? Should we sit down and weep like a lost child? Perhaps we begin to panic, and run restlessly in all directions, trying to find the way. We are paralyzed by fear of the unknown. Or else we become aggressive: Why is everything so damnably difficult?

In the Middle Ages, Dante began his *Divine Comedy* with these words:

> Halfway on the path we take through life
> I woke up and found myself in a dark wood
> with the right path lost and gone.

It was not by chance that he woke up in the middle of his life. He had been walking for half a lifetime before he opened his eyes and saw—and the path was gone.

Dante's path continued through rugged and difficult territory, full of dangers and pain. To use the language of the Middle Ages: his guide led him through hell and purgatory before he reached paradise.

Just as Dante had his guides, we too need someone to come to us on the path, someone who will walk alongside us, a guide and friend to hold our hand and calm us, one who can give us courage. We need help to see. Where are we coming from? What were we looking for? Such guides do not go in our stead, but—if we are lucky—they meet us at the critical points along the way. They accompany us for awhile and talk with us en route. Then they leave us.

Glimpses of paths and wanderings occur to me, fragments of a larger pattern. Sometimes, these are bits of the road that I myself have taken. Sometimes they are portrayed by others, but they fit into my own landscapes, since everything that is human offers us the possibility of recognition.

We shall speak here of leaving home and longing for home, the role of faith in the landscape, of drawing nearer to God and seeking to discern what one ought to be in life. For most of us, this involves a relationship to God in which both absence and presence are familiar elements.

We find all through history the motif of leaving home and longing for home. Ever since Adam and Eve were expelled from the Garden of Eden, human beings have longed to be back there. The path that leads them forward to their goal is also a path that takes them back home. The recollection of the lost paradise becomes the dream of the new paradise; the human person becomes a pilgrim. "Our heart is restless until it finds rest in you," wrote Augustine, and Bonaventure spoke of the *Itinerarium mentis in Deum*, "the soul's journey into God." Dante loses his way and is led on by another. John Bunyan wrote *The Pilgrim's*

Progress, the story of a man who departs from the city of sin and sets out on the toilsome journey toward his goal. The philosopher Gabriel Marcel spoke of the human person as *homo viator*, the "traveler."

I once saw a program on Japanese television about the development of a child before and after birth. We heard the steady rhythm of the mother's heartbeats and the quiet surge of blood through the veins. The fetus lay warm and secure in a light filtered gently through skin and tissue. In olden days, people said that the mother bore her child "under her heart." We do not remember being there, but these words can remind us of the experience of peace, of something utterly good at the origin of our lives.

Then the child emerged, since it was ready—one might almost say, "ripe." But it comes out into a colder and harder world. Simple experiments were performed on the newborn children. When they cried, the scientists played recordings of the mother's heartbeats, and the children became calm. Their weeping stopped, and harmony was reestablished. This did not last for many days, but it revealed something important about human life: after we emerge from our mother's womb, we search for a heart. Even adults sometimes take up the fetal position when they dream. There is no way backward—that would be an unhealthy regression—but the dream of a heart makes us long for something we once possessed.

To believe is to look for a heart. Religion is a longing for home. We seek our origin, the lost Eden, something present at the origin but now vanished—yet something that is not alien to us. The strange thing is that, before we can begin to search, we must discover that the path is lost. We live in the land east of Eden, and cherubim with glittering swords guard the path to the garden. We have lost the calm rhythm of the beating heart. We must feel this loss with the whole of our being before our longing leads us back.

Here, I think of the anonymous Russian pilgrim who went out into the world in the middle of his life in order to discover the meaning of the words "Pray without ceasing" (Eph 6:18). He was a pious man, and perhaps he had prayed all his life; but one day, he suddenly realized that he did not know what prayer was. *The Way of a Pilgrim* begins with these words:

> By the grace of God I am a Christian man, by my actions a great sinner, and by calling a homeless wanderer of the humblest birth who roams from place to place. My worldly goods are a knapsack with some dried bread in it on my back, and in my breast-pocket a Bible. And that is all.[2]

Bread and the Bible—food for the body and the soul of a man on his wanderings. When the meaning of life is at stake, everything else loses its significance.

I think also of one of the great intellectual geniuses in Japanese history, Kobo Daishi (774–835), a man of brilliant intelligence. Everything in life was easy for him, and he had wonderful career prospects. When he rejected power, the luxury of life at court, and a career in the bureaucracy in order to set out on his wanderings as a homeless monk, his family and friends thought he must have lost his senses, and they wanted to force him to return. But although they begged and threatened, his resolve was unshakable. "Who can break my resolve?" he said firmly. "Who can stop the wind?" He had seen through the emptiness of power and luxury. The "good life" was empty. He was whirled up from human security: he had to get out and encounter life naked.

Think of the thousands—perhaps hundreds of thousands!—of Europeans and Americans in our own days who have left home and literally become wanderers because they could no longer stand the emptiness and pretense in their own culture. They rejected the superficial life, consumerist culture, power, and violence—and often enough, they rejected a church that seemed to be swallowed up by all these intolerable factors. They walked *away* to find something they had lost. They left their childhood home because they longed to come home.

I think of an entire generation of "God's grandchildren" who were obliged to deny their parents' strict faith in order to become living human beings. They were children of people who had a profound sense of being God's children—but they had to get away, in order to find a meaning in life.

In his autobiographical *Gäst hos verkligheten* (*Guest of Reality*),[3] Swedish author Pär Lagerkvist describes his rebellion against the God of his childhood. He had to get out, he had to leave behind him the suffocating piety of his parents. But the absence left its mark on him. The mysterious One was there as a lonely attraction, as he describes it in *Aftonland* (*Sunset Land*):

Who went past my childhood's window
and breathed on it,
who went past in the deep night of childhood
where as yet no stars shine?

With his finger he traced a sign on the pane,
on the steamed-up window pane,
with the softness of his finger,
and then went on, sunk in thought.
Leaving me behind,
lonely for ever…

Who went past,
past in the deep night of childhood
and left me behind,
lonely for ever?[4]

All of Lagerkvist's poetry is an attempt to interpret the sign written by an unknown divinity on the window of the room where he lived as a child.

Let me also mention all those who do not even have a God they can deny, those who wander aimlessly around without knowing what they are seeking. Dante had lost his way in midlife, but he never doubted that there did actually exist a way, a destination, or a home. But one of Bob Dylan's songs, "Like a Rolling Stone," has stuck in my mind ever since I first heard it many years ago: in it he asks how it feels to be on your own without any direction home.

The longing certainly exists—for something, for a home, for a place to rest—but many people do not know what they are longing for. Some just wander around, without even a language that might help them formulate the object of their longings.

Some stop short and feel pain. Some feel fear, others become aggressive. For some, life seems empty. Is there any path forward? They must find something—but they do not always know what that might be.

There is one important element common to all these fragmentary landscapes: paradoxically, it appears that "wandering" becomes a conscious "seeking" only after we have lost our goal and our landmarks. Put in the language of pastoral theology: a crisis is the place where life becomes real.

Where is faith in this landscape?

Some understand faith as the sure consciousness of being at home; or else this word designates the joy they feel at having found their goal in life. While we could never wish to deprive anyone of the joy and warmth that exists in a simple and genuine faith, it is nevertheless important to emphasize that many believers are just as familiar with homelessness, absence, and yearning as they are with the certainty that God is present. What do they do, when God is hidden and the path has disappeared from sight?

We are so self-centered that we often think that it is only modern people who experience homelessness and absence. It is helpful to turn to our oldest prayer book, the Psalms of David, some of which have been in use for three thousand years. Here we find songs of praise and of lamentation, the exultant cry of gladness and the terrible cry of fear. Here faith and consolation rub shoulders with desperation and inner crises. The psalms seem familiar both with God's presence and with the darkness of his absence (Ps 42:1–3, 5):

> As a deer longs for flowing streams,
> so my soul longs for you, O God.
> My soul thirsts for God, for the living God.
> When shall I come and behold the face of God?
> My tears have been my food day and night,
> while people say to me continually,
> "Where is your God?"…
> Why are you cast down, O my soul,
> and why are you disquieted within me?
> Hope in God; for I shall again praise him,
> my help and my God.

Despite the thousands of years that separate us from these words, who can read them without recognizing the echoes of his own interior crises, his longings—and perhaps his expectations too?

Down through the years, I have often heard Christians talk about doubt and inner trials, but always in the past tense: "I myself experienced that once…When I was young…When I was studying theology…There were periods in my life when I…" They were always talking about a phase that was over. My reaction was to wonder if there were no Christians living in the depths *right now*. What strategies do they adopt? How do they survive?

There certainly are some who are in the depths. We get glimpses of them in some hymns, a sermon may hint at something of this experience, or intimate conversations may disclose a little—there is an undertone of pain, an abyss of longing, the assurance that God's absence is only the negative imprint of a much larger presence.

Let us listen to one of the church's great teachers, Anselm of Canterbury, who wrote the following words in his *Proslogion* in the eleventh century, an age when faith was strong:

> I have never seen you, Lord my God, I do not know what you look like. Highest Lord, what shall your exile do, he who comes from a distant country? What shall your servant do, who is ill at ease in his love, when he is expelled far away from your face?…You have created me and recreated me, and all the good I possess is your gift to me—and yet I do not know you. I was created to gaze upon you, but I have not yet done that for which I was created…
>
> I sought that which was good, but only confusion resulted. I yearned for God, and stumbled in my innermost heart. I sought rest in my loneliness, and found tribulation and pain deep within me. I wanted to laugh in the gladness of my soul, and I was compelled to cry out in the anguish of my heart. Joy would have been the appropriate companion of hope, but behold, endless sighing!…
>
> I will seek you in my longing and long for you in my seeking. I will find love for you, and I will love you when I find you.[5]

Strong words for a doctor of the church: "I was created to gaze upon you, but I have not yet done that for which I was created"!

In a commentary on Anselm's thought, the Danish theologian Regin Prenter notes that the atmosphere theology breathes is the inner distress caused by God's absence. This distress is not experienced by those who deny the existence of God; it is a central characteristic of the genuine search for God. Anselm was distressed by God's absence, and all true theological seeking is driven by the painful question of God's presence: "Where is your God?"[6]

Once, at a conference in Japan, I met an American psychiatrist who had worked with dying people for many years. She said that, after children, the dying are the most honest persons in the world. Their life experience could be summarized in two points: the most important things in life were "the moments and the windstorms." The "moments" were those times, rich in significance, when they succeeded in loving to the full, when they dedicated themselves and lived for others without any reservations. The "windstorms" were the periods in life when they were cast adrift in chaos and crises, when they were at risk of being whirled away by the wind or else sucked down into the depths. We had spent a whole day listening to lengthy lectures that had put us to sleep, but now our hearts began to beat afresh, for we were listening to a living person—and we met our own selves.

Inner distress is connected with the storms. No one wants them, but when they rage over our heads and we dare to enter them, they can become a decisive turning point. Inner distress is a central characteristic of the true search for God.

I have employed various metaphors to designate the object of our search: to draw nearer to God, homesickness, to look for a heart, brooks with living water, the lost paradise, our origin, the path through purgatory and hell to paradise.

Normally, all these motifs intertwine. While we look for God—or for something divine, a spring of water, "something"—we are also looking for ourselves. It is not only God who is far-away: in one way or another, we have also lost ourselves. We have put a distance between ourselves and what we were meant to be. We have forgotten what we look like, we have lost our soul. We seek the face of God, but at the same time we are seeking our own face. We are looking for the image of God in ourselves.

Henrik Ibsen's drama *Peer Gynt* can be read as a "mystery play" about the human person searching for his soul. Who is the true human being in Peer Gynt? Is he merely like an onion with layer upon layer, and no inner kernel? Or is the image of God in him? Where is the Peer who came into being in God's thoughts, as the Master wished him to be, with God's mark on his forehead?

Many who search their souls today are in fact self-centered. They hear great promises about the inner journey, about a deeper harmony, cosmic breakthroughs and higher states of consciousness, and these create immense expectations. But the path inward can be a means of escape—from other people, from the world, from God, from the existence we were meant to lead as human persons sharing the world with others.

It is important that the path inward should be part of our struggle to become what we are meant to be. Our search for God and our search for our own identity must open us up to life, so that the path inward will also be the path outward.

In my own case, the challenge was the encounter with the religiosity of the Far East. I have been privileged to meet outstanding representatives of Japanese religion in my studies, in conversations, in silence, and in meditation. They were not particularly interested in my theology, in my explanations and ideas about things: they wanted to know what was *me*—what was real in my life, what found expression in my body, the faith that lived in my movements, in my eyes, in my breathing. This was a language I had not learned. Nor were they interested in a God "out there," but in the person who was speaking. I began to realize that I could not draw closer to God without encountering my own self. Indeed, perhaps it is not too much to say that God became clear only to the extent that I dared be the person God had created me to be.

On my thirtieth birthday, I sat on a flight from Japan to Hong Kong, with thin sheets of aluminum between me and the cold outside, and with the sea 34,000 feet below me. That is more than thirty years ago now, but I still remember clearly how a simple Jewish story formulated a question for me. When Zushya was lying on his deathbed, he called his family so that he could bid them farewell and give them his blessing: "When I now cross the border and meet the Lord, he will not ask me why I was not Moses or Abraham or one of the prophets. His question will be: 'Why were you not Zushya?'"

When we seek the path that will take us deeper into faith and closer to God, we do not renounce what is human. We do indeed abandon some of our superficial longings and ambitions, our yearning for honor and our selfish dreams, and perhaps also many of the expectations and ambitions that others have on our behalf. But we do not lose touch with the deepest human dimension in ourselves. Christian faith is a process in which we take on the image we were created to bear. There is nothing in faith or in our experience to suggest that this path is easy: it can succeed only through what the Bible calls new life, a new birth, a painful process in which something must die in order that life may live.

"I was created to gaze upon you, Lord," said Anselm in the Middle Ages, "but I have not yet done that for which I was created." The first autobiographer of late antiquity, Augustine of Hippo, wrote: "You have created us for yourself, and our heart is restless until it finds rest in you." What is more natural than that the search for God's presence should also make me present in my own life?

What of our fellow wanderers? They meet us on the path, they talk with us, encourage us, warn us. Sometimes we too can offer them modest help. We cannot take the path in another's stead; we cannot solve other people's mysteries or give them a simple answer to their questions. But some of our fellow wanderers will help us to remember and to see more clearly; they will join us in searching for words to interpret what is happening. And perhaps we ourselves can point, can remind, can help others to see.

In the religious landscape, words are extremely vulnerable. They bear a meaning that can quickly become meaningless. In one instant, words that praise God can turn into mockery and cursing. The Swedish psychologist of religion Owe Wikström has given one of his books the title *De ofrånkomliga orden* (*The Inevitable Words*).[7] He speaks of words that block the path, words that are lacking, but also words that open a door.

Words block the path—everyone whose religious vocabulary has been destroyed knows this experience. Chattering preachers emptied words of their substance; the sheer weight of narrow-mindedness and oppression suffocated the words, which no longer call forth devotion, but only indignation. Nietzsche wrote: "Better songs they would have to sing to make me believe in their Redeemer: more redeemed his disciples would have to appear!"[8] Pious words shut out the landscape so that we cannot see it. The path ahead is blocked.

Words are lacking. We are beginning to grasp that some people suffer from a genuine religious aphasia, because no one has ever given them a language to use. They have no words for their unease, no words for their feelings of devotion. In an autobiographical commentary, the Norwegian author Vetle Lid Larsen wrote about the children of the 1960s' generation, who received an ample supply of resolutions and correct opinions, but no faith. He suggested that it is better to have a faith that one can perhaps reject later on than to receive no faith at all.

This is why we so desperately need words that open a door. We need keys to the doors of language, so that the divorce between words and reality can be overcome. This can happen when we set out on our wanderings with other people, following them into their various landscapes and giving them admittance to our own. In this process, words can be reborn in a living language. It is not our fellow wanderers who create these words. But they can share in the birth of new words; they can also help set old words free, so that they rise again with a new splendor. When the words open a door, we see the landscape again, and the world becomes new.

We can speak of *presence* only in images and signs. Let me borrow two images from the rich symbolic world of the Far East. Both speak of crisis and breakthrough, and both speak of presence. The first says something about the presence of other people, or perhaps rather about the interplay between the one who seeks and those with whom he speaks; the second says something about a larger presence.

Japanese Zen tradition has an eloquent metaphor for what happens in the dramatic phases of a human being's life, a religious breakthrough or an existential crisis: *sottaku doji*, "simultaneous pecking." The chick wants to get out of its egg and pecks away from within; at the same time, the hen pecks from the outside. Both must peck at the egg.

Popular wisdom adds that the pecking from within and the pecking from the outside must be coordinated: they must peck simultaneously, and the time must be right. If the hen is too eager and pecks away too soon, there is a risk that the chick may not yet be capable of surviving outside the egg; but if she pecks too late, the chick may rot in the egg.

In our striving to get out, we peck persistently. We get help from the outside, from people we meet by chance, events, conversations, meetings, or books we read. The time must be right if a viable life is to emerge from the egg. Those who wish to lead others to God have a tendency to be too eager—there is sadly such a thing as "premature faith." On the other hand, we may be so cautious that the incipient life of faith rots away. Partners in dialogue who are aware of what they can create and what they can destroy are humble in their work.

I found the other image in a book published by one of my friends, a sketchbook about the life of the novices in a Zen monastery in Japan. The book is full of vigorous life, strict discipline, hard work, and humor. One image portrays a monk who has reached his spiritual breakthrough: in an explosive moment of insight, false reality is splintered, his eyes are opened, and he can see. His body is pervaded by a vibrating presence, and he stretches out his arms in liberated exultation. At the same time, he notices something he had not seen hitherto: he is sitting on a huge hand, the hand of Buddha.

For those who know Buddhism, this is strong language. The monk had taken the Buddhist path, where nothing was given gratis, the discipline was hard as iron, and the food was poor. His life had consisted of hard work, strict meditation, sleepless nights, and perhaps brutal direction on the part of the master. The path toward insight was a life-and-death struggle. He had searched for one year, or two years, perhaps all his life. No one could take the path in his stead: he himself had to open his eyes and see. It is not for nothing that Buddhism is called the path of self-redemption.

And then one day, the breakthrough came and he saw. Life opened up, and he perceived something he had not yet known: all the time, he had been borne up by something greater, by a huge and merciful hand.

This image comes from another culture, indeed from another religion, but surely it can remind us of the deepest human insight—a divine insight—in the Christian faith. We strive and seek, we flounder and search. We lose sight of the path. We rebel, we flee, we fail in our duty, and we no longer know what it is we want. We reject our home, yet at the same time we curse our homelessness and yearn to come home. But the day our eyes are opened and we see—perhaps only in one single moment of insight—we discover that we are where we have been all the time, namely in God's hand.

The hidden presence becomes a manifest presence.

The Lost Father: Yearning for God in Our Days

More than fifty years ago, there was a total eclipse of the sun over southern Norway. We knew what would happen, so we sat and waited, with overexposed black-and-white film covering our eyes, to see the details of the sun's disappearance. Slowly, the sun was eaten up by the moon, and then it vanished. Only the radiant corona continued to glow. It was not in fact the darkness that made the greatest impression, but something we had not expected—the silence.

First came the shadow, like twilight in the middle of the day, then the brief night; all this was expected, but not the silence! The birds stopped singing, the cheerful group of people stopped talking, the world held its breath. It was not the peace of the night that descended upon us, but a paralyzing stillness. Was it the groaning of creation we heard, or the fear of emptiness, of being abandoned?

In his short book *The Eclipse of God*,[9] the Jewish philosopher Martin Buber interprets our age—the last two centuries—as a historical hour of destiny in which the sun is eclipsed. God himself is overshadowed by other phenomena.

In the silence that descends after God has vanished, philosophers seek new words, new images, new ideas that can bring him back. But Buber affirms that God is silent in the systems of the philosophers. One can dedicate oneself to ideas, perhaps even love them—but ideas do not love, so our love remains unrequited.

Buber reminds us that an eclipse is an event that takes place between the sun and our eyes, not in the sun itself. How are we to see the light again? Not by recreating it in our systems, for our words and ideas sometimes block the view, intensifying the darkness and imprisoning us in a fictional conversation with our own selves; no, we must search behind the eclipse until we find the divine mystery.

How can God once again become a reality, so that our words are more than mere sounds in the empty air? I believe that, if our yearning is to succeed in uniting words and reality, we must also take the dark silence seriously.

Let us remain in the darkness of the eclipse for a little while. I shall not attempt to explain it; instead, let us listen to three writers: Sven Delblanc, Per Olov Enquist, and Arne Garborg. Their experiences are not mine, but I can recognize the truth in what they say. They intensify the darkness, but their somber words are also nourished by a yearning for the light, for play, for birdsong, and for conversation.

Are they talking with God? I think so, although I am not always sure whether the conversation is over—or only just beginning.

Sven Delblanc's solar eclipse begins in a cornfield one beautiful autumn day in the Canada of his childhood. The golden, sweet corn is attractive. The book is called *Livets ax* (*Life's Ear of Corn*).[10] A little boy is getting to know the world by tasting and biting. The ears of corn are sweet, but they become rough and sharp; they crawl down his throat and try to strangle him. He coughs and cries out, but in vain: his father stands there and laughs uproariously, since he is a brutal, unfeeling tyrant. His sisters laugh too, since they are afraid of their father. For the screaming child, his father is a tower reaching up to the skies, mocking one who is helpless. Those who are stronger refuse to help! And then he sees the sun for the first time, hanging there like a blind face in the cloud, burning evilly, a face without eyes. He thinks: the sun is stronger than I am. The father who should have bestowed love and security gave us nothing but terror. And the sun was blind and evil.

A terrible childhood formed the picture of a world without grace. "His father had given him an image of God. Childhood had given him an image of what life was about: there were two alternatives, to lead the life of an executioner when possible, or to lead the life of a victim when compelled to do so." The blind god is the counterpart of his father. His father is the Yahweh in his life, and the son lives in his shadow.

> "I am. I am the One who is. You are only my shadow."
> I understood that he was speaking the truth—he was
> my life's Yahweh. I am his shadow. As the years pass
> and the divine evil rises to its zenith, I shall shrink
> more and more. At the last, I shall be merely a stripe
> of gray dust at his feet.[11]

What does one do when life is eclipsed by a blind and evil god who is stronger? What does one do when one is destroyed by an avenger who demands sacrifices and forgives nothing? One hangs on. The child grows up in an unchangeable world where God is eternal, his father never gets older, and terror endures. And the fate awaiting him is a rest devoid of feelings, like a fossil with staring eyes, its fear turned to stone.

But this petrified endurance in the feelingless shadow is not the whole story. His yearning and his dreams are alive. He has seen glimpses of another world: the dream of a lost paradise, fragments of faith in Jesus, and a cherry tree in bloom.

This tree is the most important factor. He discovered it on one of his wanderings away from home, a fountain of blossoms in spring, full of dark berries in summer. The tree was a friend and sister, with an important message for him: "Something about consolation in spite of everything, a message about a generous love that grows in the barrenest of soils...Only this flowering cherry tree communicated to the boy that faith in life that many a time halted his steps on the threshold to madness, as he was on the point of going out into the darkness....The stony ground was bathed in a froth, the unimagined blossoms of the fruit tree. It was like seeing God."[12] This is another God than the one he knew from his childhood home in Mölna.

The cherry tree is perhaps just another image for the dream of that lost paradise where the evil god had no power. "There existed a far-off country where his omnipotence did not reach: there, peace reigned. Only, you were expelled all too soon from that country, and this made you grieve all the more at the split in our existence." In his childhood, he had wandered unnoticed and unhindered between that realm of shadows that we call reality and the far-off land of mysticism. He longed to get back to the true reality, to the light that cast shadows on the walls of his cave.[13]

Jesus is a minor character in Delblanc's world, far too power-less to create any hope in the narrator's darkness. He could indeed recognize and understand Jesus's suffering, but he could make no sense of the idea that this suffering was meaningful! In his world, there was no place for grace and reconciliation. What weapons did Jesus possess to resist the overwhelmingly powerful blind god who enjoyed seeing human beings suffer? And Jesus never knocked on the door of his childhood home at Mölna:

> Perhaps Jesus did indeed bear the lamp of love in his hands—that was possible. But he knocked in vain on the gate of Mölna, for no one heard him, no one let

him in. The only love that still existed there was female and nature-grown like the cherry tree in the wood.[14]

Per Olov Enquist writes about a mind darkened by life. *Kapten Nemos bibliotek* (*Captain Nemo's Library*)[15] is a mysterious book on the borders between poetry and madness. Only gradually does the reader understand that we are going through an inner world that is confused and darkened. At the same time, this darkness is a place of refuge that opens up the path back to reality.

The external drama is simple. Two boys are mixed up at birth in the hospital and grow up as best friends. When they are six years old, the mistake is noticed, and they exchange homes. The newspapers write about them.

The inner drama is a callous story about what it means to be abandoned in a town in northern Sweden where people find it very difficult to express their feelings. A child loses his parents, loses the friend with whom he had been mixed up, loses his identity, loses his mind—or rather, he takes refuge in mental illness, and the reader is introduced to a part of the landscape of his mind. This is a world where imagination, recollection, and reality are woven together, but where the boy can find interconnections and perceive signals; perhaps he can even "put everything together" and create a new wholeness.

What has all this to do with God? Our initial impression is of harshness and tears—nothing else. There are only three kinds of human beings: executioners, victims, and traitors. God is overwhelming, distant, one who punishes. The human fathers are absent and dead, but nevertheless represent a threat by virtue of their very absence; the same is true of God, the highest "father." The boy had heard Mia Hallesby's[16] pious stories, which were served up to children at that time, and had understood that God was eternal. Eternity was a huge rock in the sea, where a bird flew once every thousand years to sharpen its beak. It takes an immensely long time for the rock to be completely worn down, but all that time is merely one second in eternity. And the human being fights against this overwhelming God, sharpening his beak against the rock in order to destroy it and so gain access to his Benefactor.

Hope was to be found in the Son of Man, who was not evil like God. He had a wound in his side, in which one could hide. In the local chapel, there was a picture of him and the children, with indentations in its frame. He made intercession with the divinity. "It took me all my childhood to learn that the Son of Man usually had no time—only very, very seldom."[17]

If God is a crushing eternal rock, and the Son of Man has no time, one must find other helpers. The boy's benefactor is Captain Nemo, whom he had met in one of Jules Verne's books. Captain Nemo leads him into a concealed world under the rock, with his submarine *Nautilus* as its innermost, closed room.

The name *Nemo* means "No one." In one way, both Nemo and his world are the product of a sick imagination; but it is a world that offers a place of refuge, and Nemo acts as guide to the narrator's ego, which has no identity of its own. "If one has no name, one is No one—and that too is a kind of liberation."[18]

Is this merely a story about someone who returns from the eclipse by reconstructing his life with the aid of a fictional helper? I do not think so: because en route, after more than four years in silent illness and confusion, he has perceived signals and signs.

He has come to understand that the biographies of the victims, the executioners, and the traitors are interwoven. He has perceived the clumsy, almost invisible signs of goodness in the barren society of his childhood, a society so poor in feelings. He writes without bitterness—and that in itself is a little miracle. He has seen the loneliness of the friend who became a traitor. Not least, he has grasped the abandonment and fear felt by his stepmother as she stood at the top of the stairs like a deity and destroyed her children's lives. Her fear showed him a glimpse of a deity who was different: "I saw her face when she turned toward me. Afterward, I thought: How strange that a powerful God who punishes us can be afraid of being abandoned." He had experienced something similar when he made his escape and climbed a fir tree with branches as thick as God's fingers. The branches had begun to tremble, as if God was afraid:

> One could reflect on that for a while. It had never occurred to me before now that God was afraid, but this time the fingers had trembled, just like Elma Markström's fingers—her hands were shaky. Really, it seemed that God was afraid.[19]

When I looked for a Norwegian parallel to these Swedish voices, I thought at once of Arne Garborg (1851–1924). Some consider him a rather old-fashioned writer, but he may be more modern than we think, despite all the distance in time. When he writes about human life, he has something of the intensity we find in the two Swedes. He speaks of one so wounded by life, so wounded by faith, that he had to leave home in order to seek a remedy. And yet he still longs to find a light and a meaning behind the solar darkness of his childhood religion.

In *Den burtkomne Faderen* (*The Lost Father*: the title alludes to the parable of the "lost" or "prodigal" son),[20] he writes: "I had lived like the lost son and had experienced destitution, just like him. But when I made my way home again, my father was gone. I never find peace. I am myself this unease that never comes to rest…I was a son of an age that has forgotten what 'home' and 'rest' are."

Truly,
I am not the lost son,
but you are a lost father;

and no one dares to wait for your return,
but you are missed by all your little ones.[21]

The beautiful and empty words of the church sound like a wake held over the dead Father. But here there is nevertheless one last hope: the Master.

A God?
What do we need God for?
We are perfectly capable
of condemning ourselves.
But a Son of Man
who knew us
and knew everything,
and possessed the healing word
and help
where the others merely pronounce judgments
and raise cold eyes;
a Son of Man—
oh, why are you no longer here on earth![22]

I have used fragments from the worlds of these three writers as material for my own reflections, but in doing so, I discovered that they also do something with me. They draw me into their world and make the subject matter much more difficult than I had initially thought.

Two points are particularly appropriate to this book. First, all three writers speak clearly about the pain caused when God is eclipsed. Their characters are marked by this absence, consumed by loneliness and abandonment, crushed by fear of the evil and arbitrary divinity. They hang on, they flee, or else they rebel. But will they ever escape?

Secondly, behind the pain and the flight and the rebellion lives a yearning: Garborg's search for the lost Father, which leads him to yearn for the Son of Man; Enquist's description of the helper in his imaginary world, Captain Nemo, the "No one" born of the imagination, and his glimpses of a God whose hands tremble; and Delblanc's longing for "a far-off country."

Both absence and longing are clothed in strong language. There is something universal here; we are not speaking of phenomena confined to Scandinavia at the beginning of the new millennium. When his longing reaches a breaking point, the human person returns anew to his search. The night is at its deepest just before the dawn.

Our task, then, is to speak credibly of God in a world full of distorted images of the divine. We must find something to replace the images of malicious and absent fathers and dominating mothers, something other than loneliness and guilt and repressed sexuality, something more human than power-hungry groups who so readily utter condemnations. We must speak of a God who does not crush us or force us down into the dust, but instead lets us stand upright so that we can meet him face-to-face and talk with him. Without a credible language, there is no true answer to human longings.

All this is no doubt true; but at one point, our writers disturb the clarity of our system, because they touch on something that gnaws at us and leaves us uneasy. It is not just a matter of a distorted religiosity that destroys people's emotional lives, their language, and their images of God—for Delblanc's father did not believe in God, nor did he desire to force any particular religious ideas on his son. He was merely a bad and brutal father who ruthlessly laid bare one aspect of reality, namely the cruel harshness of the world. How can we believe in a good Father, when it appears that quite different forces form human existence? Are not abandonment, violence, and heartlessness far more obvious realities than the goodness of existence? Is there any reason to believe in a good and loving Creator, rather than in a cold regularity, blind chance, or an evil power that has made the world our torture chamber? Is it not true to assert that we are abandoned? Must we not create our own world and find a benefactor, our own Captain Nemo?

If we take this reality seriously, we will not speak superficially about God.

Many Christians, however, breathe a sigh of relief in the present time: "Yes, people are truly longing! At long last, we can talk about God—and people pay attention to us. Our young people get involved in church activities. The poets and writers own up to their emptiness, the theaters take up religious problems. People are having religious experiences, they are rediscovering the Bible, they light candles in churches, they grope for words to describe their longings. There was indeed a silence after God's light was eclipsed, but the empty space is now being filled!"

We must never forget that silence too is part of the conversation; nor that the solar eclipse and the paralyzing stillness were often due to the fact that the conversation had lost all meaning. The denial and mockery of religion can be prophetic words that are far more true than many a polished affirmation about God. If the conversation does not allow this silence to be heard too, words become cheap. Garborg noted something of this truth in his novel:

> Many seek God today; and some even tell us that they have found God. I read these testimonies. But in this matter, one person cannot help another. They have had it too easy, and they write too fluently. They write and write and write. But we have so little confidence in words. We feel disturbed by everything that is said to the blast of trumpets.[23]

The solar eclipse is not experienced only by those who lack faith. Often, faith also speaks out of the same desperation, crying out to God and refusing to accept the account the Christian faith gives of him.

It was Abraham, our father in faith, who refused to accept God's terrible solution to the problem posed by the evil of Sodom and Gomorrah. He called God to account, opposing the small-mindedness of the tribal deity in the name of the divine generosity. But perhaps he fell silent when the towns were destroyed all the same? Is it not Job's protest against unjust suffering that has inspired people for more than two thousand years, rather than God's overwhelming demonstration of power, which brings Job to silence at the close of the book? In every generation, there have been Christians who had to get out, to reject the language of their tribe, and settle somewhere else. They had to bid farewell to a fossilized theology and to the pious folklore of their childhood home. Faithfulness to God required them to say no to God. They had to lose their speech and their language before they could sing a new song.

A few years ago, I read Tatiana Goricheva's little book *Talking about God Is Dangerous*. The title has a double message. It recalls that one risked one's life in the Soviet Union if one talked about God—this could lead to prison and torture. But the title indicates something even more terrible. She refers directly to her title only once in the book, when she describes the church in the West. She saw a preacher talking about love on television with smoothly practiced gestures and a polished surface. He was long-winded, empty, faceless. "For the first time," she writes, "I understood how dangerous it is to talk about God. Every word must be a word of sacrifice, full to the brim of authenticity. Otherwise, it is better to be silent."[24]

Otherwise, it is better to be silent…And yet, we speak!

What is it about faith that makes us break our silence all the time? And what makes us believe that the conversation is possible and meaningful? We are now coming near to the very center of our understanding of God, and of ourselves as human beings. In order to speak clearly, I shall employ images.

According to a Jewish legend, the world was created when God gave birth to the earth from his own body. In other words, the earth is life born of God's own life, bound to the divinity by the bonds of love and of blood. But at the same time, when the world was born, it became something completely distinct and separated from God. It was to lead its own life: it would attain a true relationship to its origin precisely by being something other than God.

I remember clearly the birth of our first child. As soon as she emerged and the umbilical cord was cut, she opened two big blue eyes that looked at us and said: "Here I am, and there you are." And we returned her gaze and saw the miracle of a new life—an infant totally dependent on our care and love, and yet the tie binding her to her mother had been cut.

A child is an autonomous living being who must find an equilibrium between nearness and distance in order to become a complete human being. We can suck the strength out of a child by binding it to us with a thousand ties; we can dominate it and overprotect it, raising it in a symbiotic relationship. But we can also cripple it by means of distance and poor care, creating a mirror image of our own inability to show feelings. In both cases, the relationship is distorted and we end up unable to communicate with each other on any meaningful level. A genuine relationship needs a wide space where child and parents can live in a free interplay. The nearness is taken for granted, but a living relationship presupposes freedom and difference. If a genuine conversation is to take place, distance is just as important as nearness.

The world is God's firstborn creation and bears the imprint of likeness to its Creator. But the umbilical cord is cut before God looks at his earth with proud and loving eyes and sees that his work is good. We must live in an open space of distance and nearness, free to form our lives and to become ourselves. Then we can encounter God face-to-face, as one distinct from our own selves, and we can talk together. The conversation needs a shared space, a relationship that binds both dialogue partners together but also presupposes their difference.

I have long been fascinated by two biblical expressions for the relationship between God and the human person: *face* and *name*.

This book speaks of the wish to find the true face of the Godhead. I have described the fear faith experiences when God's face disappears. But many are just as much afraid of an insistent nearness, of the face that looms at close quarters, seeing everything and controlling everything.

What sets us free is the presence in an open space, the blessing and peace that are imparted when the Lord lifts his face and lets the light of his face shine. Our conversation with God is now an anticipation of what Paul calls the face-to-face encounter in perfection, when we no longer see only in fragments and no longer talk like children. Our conversation trains us to approach the Godhead as fully mature persons, freed from parental authority and false ties, so that we can stand upright when we meet Him who is our origin. According to a mysterious tradition, Moses spoke face-to-face with God on the mountain, as one human being speaks with another (Exod 33:11).

The name is related to the face. For the Bible, name and reality are one: to know the name is to have power, and power may be used wrongly; but to know the name is also the basis of trust and fellowship. To know God's name is to share in God, but to misuse his name is to assault God himself.

According to the creation narrative, Adam was permitted to give names to all living beings on the earth. This implies an enormous power, for it is really the Creator who puts names to things. God calls the day light and the darkness night, he gives names to heaven and earth, he determines the number of the stars and calls each one by its name (Gen 1; Ps 147:4). When Adam put names to things, he received a share in the divine power.

In reality, trust is more important than power. Trust is the close relationship between the one who knows the name and the one who bears it, as we see clearly in the manner in which the Bible employs names. Again and again, we are told that God calls people by name: "Adam, where are you?...Your name shall be 'Abraham.'" Jacob is given the name "Israel" because he wrestled with God and won. God calls Moses, Samuel, the prophets. The Servant of the Lord is called from his mother's womb, and God has spoken his name before he was born (Isa 49:1). He has called and formed the people too: "Do not fear, for I have redeemed you; I have called you by name, you are mine" (Isa 43:1). The good shepherd calls his sheep by name. In the New Testament, the nameless are given a name: we do not know the name of the rich man who lived in luxury, but Lazarus, the beggar at his door, has a name that resounds down through the centuries (Luke 16:19–31). He is the representative of the innumerable nameless and despised persons who received life because the Master gave their names a meaning.

We say "In the name of Jesus," and there is a rich treasury of hymns and prayers that praise this name—love poetry at its finest.

Faces can be disfigured, images can be distorted until they are unrecognizable, names can be misused for evil purposes. This is the risk in every conversation. But if we refuse to take this risk, there will never be any true encounter! Trust is created when we make ourselves vulnerable and turn an unveiled face to another, waiting for his reply. The conversation gets going when one of the partners dares to trust that the other will not misuse his name, but will instead protect it.

We are formed by the images and words we use. Faces and names do something to us. It is certainly not irrelevant to ask which images of God we carry around with us; and our choice of words and names for the divine things is equally important. Do we evoke the radiant face of blessing, or the blind god, the stern father who mocks the helpless? God's eye can be full of concern, an eye that neither slumbers nor sleeps. But it can also be Garborg's divinity, who watched over him "with eyes of fire," so that he had to escape in order to know gladness. Or it can be the Son of Man who "possessed the healing word / and help / where the others merely pronounce judgements / and raise cold eyes." Or it can be a divinity who is the eternal rock that blocks the path to our benefactor.

We have tried out a number of images and words: face to face; the name that calls to another name; the umbilical cord is cut and the child meets its own origin as *Another*. Many people criticize Christianity for directing its faith to something outside the human person, thereby depriving us of our autonomy. There is something correct in this charge, but it is basically wrong, since the point is not that we *localize* faith somewhere else and seek an object "out there." The important thing is the relationship, the interconnection. Faith lives in the space between, that is, in what we call trust, conversation, encounter, and love.

When we keep on breaking the silence and speaking, this is not because we have adequate words to describe God or to speak to him, but because conversation is the innermost essence of faith in God. If the divine had been a set of rules inherent in the world, an idea, or an impersonal divine force permeating all things—including the deepest dimension in our own being—then we could perfectly well have remained silent, as in some forms of mysticism, which rest in the realm of the unutterable. Enter your own sanctuary, they say, and remain in the silence; words are superfluous, since you yourself are the divine. Here there is no face for us to meet, no Other with whom we can converse, only unity with our own innermost self.

In the Christian faith, I encounter Another, a face and a name that are not my own. This is my origin, but the umbilical cord has been cut. I must grow apart from my mother's womb and my father's embrace, learning to straighten my back and stand face-to-face.

We too can remain silent as we stand before the divine mystery; words are obviously inadequate. But the silence will always be broken, just as a man and woman who love one another will always grope for words to express their love, however poorly. In the same way, friends cannot remain silent. The beloved one has a face.

How can we speak credibly about the object of our faith? How can language be recovered, and the words arise from the dead?

"We must pull up our socks," think the preachers—and get a bad conscience. "We must improve our formulations, discover new images, seek inspiration in poetry and literature, speak with greater commitment, draw on art for help…"

Rhetoric and beauty are certainly important, but I have come to believe that the vital thing is not our ability to formulate or our rhetorical skill, but the *space* in which our words are heard, and not least the space that our words create. We must help people to experience faith anew as an open space, a landscape they can enter, where they will receive a language by hearing and speaking, seeing, and experiencing. But they need fresh air around them in this landscape, and they must be free to leave again.

People are accustomed to see faith as something ministers and preachers want to force down their throats: a system, a language, a whole world of opinions that they must accept. The words are weapons launched against them, seeking their weak points. They are meant to sting like salt in open wounds, giving them a bad conscience. The goal is to bring them to conversion. But they get claustrophobia and then retreat, since there is no place for their own reality in the words' closed room. The church's language reminds them too much of authorities that seek control, of parents who cannot let go of their children.

If language is to live, it must be formed in a vast space, large enough to accommodate the whole of life. It must be tested in longing and rebellion. It must have depths in which both blasphemy and adoration can resonate—and desperation, fear, and exultation. Abraham could quarrel with God because he inhabited a huge universe of faith. Job and the prophets shook their fists at God and cursed the day of their birth because they needed fresh air around them. Language must be heard in a vast room of faith that people can enter without feeling imprisoned. Perhaps such a room will make it possible for them to really commit themselves!

Some people have to go so far away that the last remaining bit of the umbilical cord breaks, before they come as adults to long for another kind of conversation, and try to pick up the threads once more. Perhaps the god who breathed fear and coldness into them may turn out to have loving qualities. There must also be space for the "foreigners" who want to try out a language they have never learned. In this way, faith can become a voyage of discovery, on which their lives are given a place in a larger landscape with new dimensions and new joys—though assuredly, there will be hitherto unknown abysses as well.

Ultimately, it is the gospel stories about Jesus that open up the landscape and sketch a face of God that allows us to believe that our longing can actually lead somewhere.

It is not by chance that Jesus was a wanderer—from one village to another in Galilee's mountain landscape, with their pastures and small fields, on streets and market squares, and in the wildernesses where no one lived. Around him, a whole world took form. People were drawn into a reality that was utterly close yet different and new—a reality he called "the kingdom of God." This was not a place, but a path and a landscape that they were permitted to share by following him and trying it out for themselves.

The Gospels speak of very simple matters: Jesus meets people and talks with them, touches them, blesses them, eats with them, heals, weeps, speaks about life's mysteries and about God. They had indeed heard about this, but now it was here! The path also went to Jerusalem, where it seemed that Jesus's world was collapsing—the king in the kingdom of God received a gallows as his throne. In his world, God was the highest and the lowest. Heaven and hell were God's place.

The Jesus of the Gospels is not a nice but powerless reconciler, with no weapons to challenge the divinity who was an "eternal rock." The Jesus of the Gospels is not an absent figure who never dared to knock on the door, because a brutal father and a blind god were all too much alive for him. No, in the Gospels it is the Highest himself who visits the earth. God makes his way through narrow lanes and back alleys and says: "Let there be light!" Eyes that were dulled become bright; people straighten up. Those who had been despised are given back their names, and the sinners receive a face.

If *this* is the face of God, then we can straighten up and try to speak. The Almighty has a human countenance. This is a God whose hands tremble, to borrow Enquist's image: "It had never occurred to me before now that God was afraid...Really, it seemed that God was afraid." This is a God whose image is reflected in the fear felt by the victims—and by the executioners and the traitors. What other founder of a religion was terror stricken and cried out: "Now is my soul full of fear" (John 12:27)?

Jesus's life and death—his failure, in human terms—were not a sacrifice demanded by a harsh God, nor were they the defeat of a well-meaning idealist. No, they were made of the same stuff as life itself. Those who ruled were able to take power and honor from Jesus, for he himself had already laid such things aside; but they could not take life and love from him.

Perhaps, in the final analysis, something of this Jesus was revealed in the glimpses of life and of meaning in Delblanc's gloomy world: the fruit tree in the abandoned smallholding that bloomed unseen in the dark forest and told him "something about consolation in spite of everything, a message about a generous love which grows in the barrenest of soils...It was like seeing God"!

What I have written about the relationship to God implies that the meeting between God and the human person takes the form of a conversation. This relationship is nourished by words, develops in words, and is shaped by words. The intensity varies, and there is an alternation between distance and closeness; words may be many or few. And it is certainly true that the spoken word is not the only form of expression! Nevertheless, faith seeks words.

It may be tempting to reflect on the consequences that this basic relationship to God has for the language of theology and of preaching, but I content myself here with one single affirmation. One element in the crisis in theology and preaching is that they have become detached from the fundamental language of conversation, the conversation that takes the form of prayer, lamentation, and hymns of praise, cries of fear and of joy, accusation and protest, the longing of the abandoned lover, the intimate dialogue, the poetry of love, and the silence that simply waits for the other.

The language of preaching and theology is not of course this direct conversation itself. But its language is without passion when it loses contact with the experiences and insights we derive from the direct conversation. The words become abstract, lifeless, and tedious.

We must return briefly to one point, which was taken up in the introduction to this section: the solar eclipse, the silence after God disappears. For it is not only ideas that put God in the shadow; it is not only distorted images of God and a ruined language that reduce us to silence. We can solve such problems by renewing our language and painting other images. But what are we to do when the eclipse is caused by the brutality of reality itself, when we are plagued in our hearts by the absence of light and of goodness, when it seems that darkness reigns?

Faith has no solution to this, nor any genuinely satisfactory answer; nevertheless, it answers in the inner distress. It answers by speaking. The biblical answer is protest, the cry of anguish, accusation, and expectation—"How long? Have you forgotten us? Have you forgotten who you are, O God?" Faith speaks because it goes deeper than the inner distress and is nourished by hope's defiance. Many factors can block our view, dull our eyes, and spread the contagion of hopelessness. At the beginning of the twenty-first century, it is impossible for us to profess the optimistic faith in divine providence that came so naturally to earlier generations, whose life was successful but who perhaps saw less. A thousand truths assault our faith in God's goodness, which is full of contradictions and as vulnerable as a little child in the thick of battle.

This is why we continue to speak. Hope must be proclaimed, hope must be repeated as a protest. We must urge people to hope, setting up a bulwark against pessimism and all the forces that destroy life. We must remind one another unceasingly of the signs that point to the deepest forces in life and are stronger and truer than the signs that point to annihilation.

In the depths, our words of hope draw their nourishment from faith in a God whose hands tremble, who is familiar with abandonment, a God who resembles the cherry tree defiantly blossoming unseen on barren ground, a God who has a face like the Son of Man.

> But a Son of Man
> who knew us
> and knew everything,
> and possessed the healing word
> and help
> where the others merely pronounce judgments
> and raise cold eyes;
> a Son of Man—
> oh, why are you no longer here on earth!

Garborg was right to reject the overwhelming, power-hungry Father. If he had persevered in his search, his appreciation of the Son of Man might perhaps have restored the Father to him. The reader perceives this possibility in the silent wonder at the close of Garborg's novel: "If I could live a few more years, and lead a new life, I believe that I could still find the Father."[25]

NOTES

Preface: Toward a Greater Faith

1. Notto R. Thelle, *Hvem kan stoppe vinden? Vandringer i grenseland mellom Øst og Vest [(Who Can Stop the Wind? Travels in the Borderland Between East and West)]* (Oslo: Oslo University Press, 1991, 4th–6th printing by Oriens Publishing Company).

I. The Light of the Face

1. Abraham Heschel, *Man Is Not Alone* (New York: The Jewish Publication Society of America, 1951), 91.

2. Sadao Watanabe (1913–1996) is a Japanese artist who has used the Japanese art form of stencil printing to express Biblical themes in unique ways.

3. I received the poem on a fax and have not been able to find the author.

4. Tomas Tranströmer, *För levande och döda* (For the Living and the Dead) (Stockholm: Bonniers, 1989), 26.

5. Martin Buber, *The Eclipse of God* (New York: Harper & Row, 1952), 6–9.

6. Knut Hamsun, *Victoria* (Kristiania/Oslo: Gyldendalske bokhandel, 1922), 31.

7. Kosuke Koyama, *Waterbuffalo Theology* (London: SCM Press, 1974).

II. Face to Face

1. I have been unable to locate the quotation, which I once wrote down from one of Jens Bjørneboe's essays.

2. Vaclav Havel, quoted in Norwegian newspapers during the conference in Oslo, September 17, 1990.

3. Kenneth Cragg, *Sandals at the Mosque: Christian Presence Amid Islam* (London: SCM Press, 1959).

4. Ibid., 137–38.

5. Kosuke Koyama, *Mount Fuji and Mount Sinai: A Critique of Idols* (Maryknoll, NY: Orbis Books, 1974), 260.

6. Kazoh Kitamori, *Theology of the Pain of God* (Richmond, VA: John Knox Press, 1965), 119; I have translated directly from the Japanese original, *Kami no itami no shingaku* (1947; repr., Tokyo: Shinkyo Shuppansha, 1972), 182.

7. Jean Sulivan, *Morning Light: The Spiritual Journey of Jean Sulivan*, trans. Joseph Cunneen and Patrick Gormally (New York: Paulist Press, 1988), 13.

8. Sven Delblanc, *Grottmannen* (Stockholm: Bonniers, 1977), 8.

9. Axel Jensen, *Ikaros* (1957; repr., Oslo: Cappelen, 1986), 106.

10. Pär Lagerkvist, *Ahasverus död* (Stockholm: Bonniers, 1960), 127.

11. Pär Lagerkvist, *Aftonland* (Stockholm: Bonniers, 1953), 59.

12. Anders Frostenson, "Guds kärlek är som stranden och som gräset," in *Den svenska psalmboken*, 4th ed. (Örebro, Sweden: Libris förlag, 1986), no. 289.

13. I have been unable to locate the quotation, which I had written down from one of Jens Bjørneboe's essays.

14. Source unknown, quoted after memory.

15. Dietrich Bonhoeffer, *Nachfolge*, trans. Stephan Tschudi, from the Norwegian *Lydighetens vei* (Oslo: Land og Kirke, 1956), 81–82.

16. Quoted from the Swedish original *Vägmärken* (Stockholm: Bonniers, 1963), 73.

17. The poem is quoted from a photocopied leaflet from 1979. For the struggle against the oppressive regime of president Park Chung Hee and Kim Chi Ha's involvement, see Kim Chi Ha, *The Gold-Crowned Jesus & Other Writings* (Maryknoll, NY: Orbis Books, 1978).

18. Ibid.

19. *A Thousand Reasons for Living*; quoted from the Norwegian edition, *Tusen grunner til å leve* (Oslo: Verbum, 1985), October 8, 1974.

III. Out of the Depths

1. Finn Bjørnseth, *Logos* (Oslo: Gyldendal, 1972), 57.

2. *The Way of a Pilgrim*, trans. R.M. French (New York: The Seabury Press, 1965), 1.

3. Pär Lagerkvist, *Gäst hos värkligheten* (1925; repr., Stockholm: Bonniers, 1960).

4. Pär Lagerkvist, *Aftonland*, 46–47.

5. *Proslogion*, chapter 1, quoted from Danish in Regin Prenter, *Guds virkelighed* [*The Reality of God*] (Fredricia: Lohses Forlag, 1982), 17.

6. Ibid., 79.

7. Owe Wikström, *De ofrånkomliga orden* (Stockholm: Gummesson, 1982).

8. Friedrich Nietzsche, *Also sprach Zarathustra*, quoted after the Norwegian translation, *Slik talte Zarathustra*, trans. Amund Hønningstad (Oslo: Gyldendal, 1962), 58.

9. Martin Buber, *The Eclipse of God* (New York: Harper & Row, 1952), 22–24.

10. Sven Delblanc, *Livets ax* (Stockholm: Bonniers, 1991).

11. Ibid., 101.

12. Ibid., 60–61.

13. Ibid., 182–83.

14. Ibid., 175.

15. Per Olov Enquist, *Kapten Nemos bibliotek* (Stockholm: Norstedts Förlag, 1991).

16. Mia Hallesby was a prolific Norwegian writer of devotional books for children. Her husband, Ole Hallesby, was a conservative theologian and aggressive revivalist preacher, internationally known for his book on prayer.

17. Enquist, *Kapten Nemos bibliotek*, 8–9.

18. Ibid. 9.

19. Ibid., 223–24

20. Arne Garborg, *Den burtkomne Faderen* (1899; repr., Oslo: Aschehoug 2001), 101.

21. Ibid., 129.

22. Ibid., 132.

23. Ibid., 115.

24. I quote from the Norwegian edition, Tatiana Goricheva, *Farlig å tale om Gud* (Ottestad: Prokla-Media, 1989), 106.

25. Garborg, *Den burtkomne Faderen*, 151.